12 RULES FOR A CHRISTIAN LIFE

DISCOVERING REAL LIFE IN THE PRACTICES AND PRIORITIES OF JESUS

CHRIS GREER

Here's to discovering
real life as we walk
in the light! (John 8:12)

M
STREET

12 Rules for a Christian Life: Discovering Real Life in the Practices and Priorities of Jesus

Published by M-Street Publishing

Print ISBN: 978-1-956439-00-7

eBook ISBN: 978-1-956439-01-4

Copyright © 2021 by Chris Greer. All rights reserved.

Cover design by Vanessa Mendozzi

Contact Chris Greer directly at chris@chris-greer.com to schedule author appearances and speaking events.

CONTENTS

Invitation   v

Preface: A Letter   ix

Introduction   1

PART I
RULES FOR LIFE WITH GOD

1. Fight For Space   15
2. Listen To Jesus   35
3. Read The Bible...Slowly   53
4. Become A Mystic   73

PART II
RULES FOR LIFE WITH OTHERS

5. Join The Church   95
6. Don't Just Sing There   115
7. Give Yourself Away   133
8. Redefine Love   151

PART III
RULES FOR LIFE WITH YOURSELF

9. Remember Who You Are   175
10. Name Your Idols   195
11. Embrace Your Suffering   215
12. Share The Gospel   237

Epilogue   259

More for the Journey   265
Acknowledgments   267
Appendix   271
Notes   281

INVITATION

Purposeful. Meaningful. Satisfying. Real.

It's the kind of life we all want to live.

And *it's possible...*

That's what this book—and everything Chris Greer and M-Street Publishing produces—is about.

Find free resources and get updates at www.Chris-Greer.com.

Visit.
Sign up.
And let's *live.*

For Jacob and Emma, two of God's greatest gifts.

There is much your mom and I can teach you, but none of it matters more than what's in this book.

PREFACE: A LETTER

Dear Reader,

I still remember walking through a tiny bookstore in Columbia, Tennessee when a bestselling book—*12 Rules for Life* by Jordan Peterson—caught my eye. Before even picking it up, this question popped into my mind: What are the 12 rules for a *Christian* life?

Not long after, while making space to listen, God impressed on me that this book—*12 Rules for a Christian Life*—was my next writing assignment.

Many years before that, I was a boy raised in a Christian family by parents who loved and followed Jesus with their own set of Rules for life. Through their example and leadership, God impressed upon me that he was worth paying attention to.

Unfortunately, as I entered young adulthood, I paid far more attention to the black-and-white "rules" of religion than I did the life-giving rhythms of divine relationship. I entered college as a frustrated, legalistic law-keeper who was far from God, ignorant of the way of Jesus, and closed off to the winsome wind of the Holy Spirit.

Thankfully, God was not content with that. And he refused to leave me alone.

Through the lives of two fellow freshmen—Jerry and Keely—God showed me what a real, dynamic, and authentically human relationship with Jesus could be. Their walk with Jesus blew my mind. I saw in them, my new friends, what I took for granted in my faithful parents.

They were living *real* life.

And I wanted to live it too.

For the first time I became interested in the ways of God rather than just the laws of God, and with others' help, I began pursuing the kinds of habits included in this book. I tiptoed into practices like reading the Bible slowly, listening for Jesus, and participating with his people.

One of the things Jesus soon communicated to me was this: "Chris, I've pursued you for a long time. Now it's *your turn* to pursue *me*." I remember it like it was yesterday; God ignited in me a new desire to speak his name out of intimate relationship, not out of religious obligation.

That changed everything.

Life is an uneven road. Sometimes I'm a pretty good driver, but at other times I've been the at-fault party in some pretty nasty crashes.

Like you, I've experienced much of what the world has to offer, and let's be honest, it's just not enough. The most common pursuits rarely lead to an uncommon life. So, I live Jesus' way, by the power of his Spirit and all the effort I can muster, and I'm growing to want nothing more than him.

I've lived in small towns and big cities in the Deep South and the West Coast. I've attended public schools and a private seminary. I was single for a long time and now married a while.

Professionally, I've worked jobs as a college admissions counselor, a waiter, a tour guide, an administrative assistant, a pastor (a few times), a screen-printer, a small business-owner, and a writer (to list only some of my favorites).

Spiritually, I've learned the ropes from my wife, friends, family members, colleagues, pastors, seminary professors, mentors, authors, and preachers.

I have a long way to go. But I've also come a long way. And I want you and everyone I know to come with me.

Because it's in relationship with God—through Jesus—that real human life is found.

Here's to God, to you, and to a life well lived through these practices and priorities of Jesus, the 12 Rules for a Christian life.

Onward,
  Chris Greer

INTRODUCTION

"The Christian ideal has not been tried and found wanting. It has been found difficult; and left untried."
—G.K. Chesterton

We are a peculiar people.

On one hand, we dislike rules and recoil at being told what to do. Yet on the other, few of us live without structure.

We prize autonomy and clamor for unrestricted "freedom," but every last one of us submits to a rule-laden paradigm.

We are disciplined, even when we pretend to be unfettered.

We crave organization, even when we claim to desire unbridled spontaneity.

The reality is no human being survives, much less thrives, without a set of boundaries that govern his or her thoughts and actions. We may bristle at the mention of "rules," but we don't dare live without them.

So, when it comes to the word "rules" the only intellectually honest questions to ask are which set do you live by and why.

The word "Christian" is also shrouded with ambiguity in Western culture. Some still consider America a Christian country, yet fewer and fewer of her citizens identify as such.[1] Some count Sunday church attendance as the baseline for Christian living while others believe following Jesus entails far more than that.

Consequently, a shared definition for the two words—Rules and Christian—will prove helpful. Understanding both is central to everything you will read in this book. So let's begin with Rules.

12 Rules

There are rules, and then there is a Rule.

Rules are black-and-white, hard-and-fast boundary markers designed to keep order. They delineate right from wrong, who's in or out, and what can and cannot happen. Another word for these sorts of rules is "laws."

The Bible certainly contains laws, but far too many people assume that Christianity is about nothing more than who keeps them and who doesn't.

Moral laws are necessary and good, but they're different from the Rules I write about here. These Rules for a Christian life are disciplines. They're practices, habits, and routines that provide scaffolding for a way of living, not just a list of things to do. They are tried and true, but not necessarily black and white.

These twelve practices and priorities of Jesus usher us into a way of being that makes life grow and flourish. They take us where we most long to go, helping us become who we most need to become.

These Rules are nothing short of a roadway to a rich and satisfying life with God.[2]

Practicing To Be Human

In his best-selling book *Outliers,* journalist Malcolm Gladwell wrote about the ten-thousand-hour phenomenon. Researchers believe it takes ten thousand hours of sustained practice at any trade, skill, or discipline to master it or become an expert.

No doubt the likes of Stephen King, Misty Copeland, Adele, Serena Williams, Steph Curry, Steve Jobs, and Malcolm Gladwell practiced their craft for the requisite ten thousand hours. And they are just a few famous ones.

Every accomplished surgeon, teacher, accountant, interior designer, fisherman, furniture maker, potter, dentist, biologist, pastor, and parent can attest to the truth that "practice isn't the thing you do once you're good. It's the thing you do that makes you good."[3]

Every expert—well known or not—reached the highest levels of expertise and experience by adhering to a specific way of life, a paradigm of practices, a list of disciplines. On the road to mastery, each developed a dynamic but structured Rule for Life.

Now imagine if the goal was to excel at being human rather than simply mastering a skill or trade.

What if the object was to become an expert at living the fullest, deepest, and most fulfilling life possible? What set of practices and disciplines—which Rules—would you adopt to realize that lofty goal?

If there was a framework for living the most fruitful existence possible, would you want to know it? Would you be interested in the "rules" that make that kind of life possible?

If you are, then you've found the right book.

A Rule for Life

The adoption of a particular set of spiritual disciplines is what Christians for centuries have referred to as a "Rule" or a Rule for Life.

The leaders of Bridgetown Church in Portland, Oregon, describe a Rule for Life like this: "A Rule for Life is a ...set of practices and relational rhythms that help us create space in our busy world for us to be with Jesus, become like Jesus, and do what he did."[4]

These 12 Rules are practices and relational rhythms to help you focus on Jesus and become like him by doing what he did. Each Rule is a habit that leads to transformation.

Look closely at what Jesus did and said and you'll find that he lived according to his own Rule for Life and taught everyone who followed him to do the same. And he began with the greatest rule of all.

The Greatest Rule

Some of the first-century Jewish "teachers of religious law"[5] asked Jesus again and again about his interpretation of their religious rules. They aimed to trip him up with their law-based line of questioning so they could dismiss and discredit him as a breaker of God's laws.

But Jesus elevated the conversation. He pointed them beyond religious dogma.

When asked to articulate the most important of all God's instructions, Jesus answered with his Rule for Life.

> Jesus told them, "The most important commandment is this: 'Listen, O Israel! The Lord our God is the one and only Lord. And you must love the Lord your God with all your heart, all your soul, all your mind, and all your strength.' The second is equally important: 'Love your neighbor as yourself.' No other commandment is greater than these." (Mark 12:29-31)

This was broader and better than a simple law and more grand and comprehensive than a single rule.

The most important command was, and is, a Rule for Life. It's the way to live life in a thriving relationship with God, others, and oneself.

And that is the point of this book. These 12 Rules comprise a Rule for Life that will help you live out Jesus' Great Commandment. They will lead you into real life with God, others, and yourself, and open the door for the Spirit of God to enliven you like never before.

Now that we have a definition for the word "Rules," let's address the word "Christian."

A Christian Life

Each year Barna, a research and polling firm, publishes its "State of the Church" report. For the purpose of understanding their poll results, Barna classifies practicing Christians as those who "identify as Christian, agree strongly that faith is very important in their lives and have attended church within the past month."[6]

Barna's work is important and helpful, but it's important to understand that self-identifying as a Christian, believing faith is important, and attending Christian gatherings do not make you a Christian. Nor does adherence to Christian morals or applying all 12 Rules in this book.

Each of these is a crucial part of being a Christian, but they don't make you one.

So what *does* it mean to be Christian? Thankfully, it's not guesswork. The Bible tells us what it means to be a Christian.

According to the Bible, the ideal human life is a relationally connected one, not a religiously observant one. The teaching of Jesus—in harmony with all of Scripture[7]—helps us understand what that means, beginning with one of his most famous lines of all.

God Loves the World So Much

John 3:16 is one of the most quoted Bible verses in Christendom. Jesus spoke those well-known words during a one-on-one conversation with Nicodemus, a first-century religious leader who knew there was more to Jesus than met the eye.[8]

As they spoke, Jesus reordered Nicodemus' religious paradigm. Jesus wanted Nicodemus to understand that real human life begins when you are "born from above."[9]

That phrase bewildered Nicodemus as much as it does people today. But simply put, being born from above is to be reborn spiritually. God desires for all human beings to enter into a life that is deeply spiritual, not just material.

As their conversation continued, Jesus spoke these memorable words. He said,

> For God so loved the world that he gave his one and only Son,
> that whoever believes in him shall not perish but have eternal life.
> (John 3:16 NIV)

These twenty-six English words encapsulate God's core message about himself, his son Jesus, and what is possible for all humanity because of his great love for us.

What it means to be Christian begins with this good news: God loves you and all his creation so much that he sent Jesus to redeem every part of it and provide eternal life for all who believe.

And that good news is even better than most folks think.

This Is Eternal Life

A common misconception is that the point of Christianity is a never-ending, pleasure-filled existence in a place called Heaven. But eternal life is better than just living forever in paradise.

Eternal life is being united—in the deepest, most satisfying relationship—with the God of the universe.

Read that sentence again slowly.

Spend some time silently pondering the miracle of true unity with God, if you can.

Because *that* is what Jesus talked about.

That is what God desires.

That is what Jesus made possible.

That is where authentic human life is found.

Here's proof. Just moments before Jesus' arrest and crucifixion, he expressed to God the Father his deepest desires for you and me. He prayed that all who follow him would receive "eternal life."[10] Then he stated exactly what eternal life is.

> Now this is eternal life: that they know you, the only true God, and Jesus Christ, whom you have sent. (John 17:3 NIV)

Did you catch it? We don't have to guess what eternal life is because Jesus defined it, and it's far more than just going to Heaven when we die.

Eternal life, according to the Son of God, is *knowing God and Jesus Christ, whom God sent.*

Let me repeat what I wrote above: The ideal human life is not a religiously observant one, it's a relationally connected one.

To be Christian is to *know God*, thanks to Jesus.

From the start of creation to the culmination of history, God's mission is to reunite his precious humans with himself. Even in spite of our sustained rebellion, God loves us and pursues us in the great hope that we will once and for all say "yes!" to him. He longs for us to receive his grace and enter into deep and lasting union with him.

And that divine union is what makes us children of God. It's what makes us Christian.

People don't become Christians by keeping a set of rules, attending certain gatherings, or believing the right set of doctrinal statements. We become Christian when we are unified with God through Jesus Christ and filled by his Holy Spirit.

And the deeper we go with him, the more human we become, as we will see in the next words of Jesus.

Saving Is Losing, Losing Is Saving

All four of the Gospel books in the Bible—Matthew, Mark, Luke, and John—include another declaration of Jesus that helps us fully understand what it means to be Christian.

> Calling the crowd to join his disciples, he said, "If any of you wants to be my follower, you must give up your own way, take up your cross, and follow me. If you try to hang on to your life, you will lose it. But if you give up your life for my sake and for the sake of the good news, you will save it." (Mark 8:34-37)

Jesus pulled no punches. Following him is no joke. It's not a lighthearted, fair-weather, partial commitment. It's not easy or without sacrifice.

True union with God is serious and all consuming.

But as counterintuitive as it seems, it's also completely *freeing*.

The key is Jesus' promise. When we live our life on our terms rather than his, we lose out. Big time. But those who trade their own way, preferences, and self-focused desires for a fully devoted, sold-out, and obedient life with him are saved. They are made whole, and they gain *everything*.

There are plenty of notions about what it means to be human, but Jesus sets the record straight. Human beings are meant to be relationally united with God, and anyone who lives a life disconnected from him lives a partial, less than fully human life.

Last but not least, Jesus' Greatest Commandment rounds out

the true definition of a Christian life. Let's take a look before we jump into the 12 Rules.

What Christians Do

Christians are folks who are united with God as they recognize his love, trust Jesus' death on their behalf, and receive God's forgiveness for their sin. Out of gratitude and humility, they willingly give up their own way and discover—by the Holy Spirit's power—true human life in their union with God.

That's who Christians are. Now here's what Christians do. Again, in the words of Jesus...

The most important commandment is this... "You must love the Lord your God with all your heart, all your soul, all your mind, and all your strength." The second is equally important: "Love your neighbor as yourself." No other commandment is greater than these. (Mark 12:29-31)

Enabled by their union with God, Christians devote everything they are and have to God, and they love everyone else like they love themselves.

This is what it means to be Christian, and learning to live this way is the heart and soul of *12 Rules for a Christian Life*. In accordance with the most important of all God's commands, the Rules that follow will help you remain united with God, love others well, and live the one true life he intended.

How This Works

Now that we've defined the words "Rules" and "Christian," here's what you can expect the rest of the way.

12 Rules for a Christian Life is organized according to Jesus' Great Command. The first four Rules are Rules for life with God. The second four Rules are for life with others. The final four Rules are for life with yourself. Each Rule is drawn from Jesus' practices and priorities as written for us in the Gospels.

Each chapter concludes with a description of how I engage God through that Rule. Dialing in these practices has been a multi-year process, but rest assured I'm still on the journey. Like you, my relationship with Jesus is a work in progress.

I can tell you this: Discovering your real life through the practices and priorities of Jesus will take significant effort and time. It's not easy. It requires testing, reflection, and commitment. But it can be done, and you can do it. And *real* life with God is the result.

I share my personal practices so you can learn from them, adopt them, or use them as a primer for designing your own practice for that particular Rule.

Throughout the book, I use the words God, Jesus, and Holy Spirit almost interchangeably. In each case I am referring to the God of the Bible who is the Trinity—the one true God in three persons, existing eternally in perfect union and community.

Each person—God the Father, God the Son (Jesus), and God the Spirit (Holy Spirit)—is distinct, yet each is God, so I refer to all three persons as I encourage you to engage with him throughout the 12 Rules.[11] This is particularly true in Rule #2, Listen to Jesus.

Last, I encourage you to do three things as you read.

First, keep your Bible close by. Look up the quoted Scripture passages for yourself and highlight or take notes in the margins of your Bible. This will prove fruitful when you return to those verses in the future.

Second, pay attention to the practices, but don't try to adopt all of them immediately. The epilogue includes a plan for slowly integrating these Rules, and God will guide you to the right Rule and practice for your next steps with him.

My final encouragement is one you will be tempted to ignore. But ironically, it is the most crucial.

Read and practice the 12 Rules *with others*.

We're all tempted to individualize our faith. But as you will discover in Rule #5, God designed Christians to walk with Jesus together, not alone.

Invite a few close friends, some colleagues, your spouse, a mentor, a fellow student, or a group in your church to invest twelve weeks—one for each Rule—together. Explore and engage the Rules with God and each other and he will enrich all your lives significantly. That's a promise.[12]

———

The world is fast, but life with God is slow.

The world starves us, but God nourishes us.

I invite you to slow down, to rest, and to take the Rules one at a time.

Finally, I invite you to receive Jesus' invitation as worded in *The Message*:

> Are you tired? Worn out? Burned out on religion? Come to me. Get away with me and you'll recover your life. I'll show you how to take a real rest. Walk with me and work with me—watch how I do it. Learn the unforced rhythms of grace. I won't lay anything heavy or ill-fitting on you. Keep company with me and you'll learn to live freely and lightly. (Matthew 11:28-30 MSG)

May God bless you immensely and fill you with his Spirit as you work your way through *12 Rules for a Christian Life.*

PART I

RULES FOR LIFE WITH GOD

The most important commandment is this: "*...You must love the Lord your God with all your heart, all your soul, all your mind, and all your strength.*"

The second is equally important: "Love your neighbor as yourself." No other commandment is greater than these."

— Jesus (Mark 12:29-31)

1

FIGHT FOR SPACE

"There are huge benefits in leaving the center of things and going off into the margins."
—David Brooks

If you asked some friends or colleagues to give an hour-by-hour description of their average day, what would you hear?

One guy starts his day at 5:30 a.m., another begins at nine. One woman goes to bed at midnight while another dons her eye mask no later than 8:45 p.m. The start and end times would vary, but the time spent between would likely sound very similar.

Workdays are jammed with meetings and briefings, zoom calls and sales calls, teaching and learning, driving and delivering, preparing and presenting. Then time at home is full of conversations and coordination, cooking dinner and caring for kids. Even weekends are chock full of to-do lists and obligations.

Sharing a rundown of your daily rituals pulls back the curtain on a common theme: everyone's days are packed. The details differ, but the overall program is the same.

Work—even work you enjoy—is a race. Sometimes it's a runaway train. There's more to do than can be done in a single day. The meetings, presentations, consultations, travel, research, appointments, and emails demand more and more of your time.

Every hour—or less—you skate from one task to another. Various personal or electronic interruptions pop up throughout the day as your mind shifts from project to project.

In the background, music plays, a podcast talks, a television flickers. And in every crack between, no matter how small, you instinctively fidget with your device. Your hands and eyes—not to mention your mind and soul—dart from notification to notification, stealing every free moment.

The description of our day-to-day existence is exhausting to read. It's even more exhausting to live. And why? Because there's very little...

...*S P A C E.*

Is More, More?

"Less is more" is a well-known idiom, but few believe it. In reality, most of our lives are not-so-subtle declarations that we believe *more* is more. The proof is in the way we think and talk about busyness. We wear our busyness like a badge of honor.

A million times a day the question "How are you?" receives the response, "Good! Things are busy!" We want others to believe our life is cranking along at breakneck speeds just like theirs, and we couldn't be happier about it! Meanwhile our EKG results, panic attacks, and emergency therapy sessions tell a different story.

I once asked the pat question—"Staying busy?"—to an acquaintance and was shocked by his answer. He replied, "Sadly, yes." Then his tone and eyebrows lifted as he said, "But I'm working to change that. I won't be busy forever."

I wasn't sure whether to roll my eyes at his out-of-touch response or hug him. It was shocking, yet refreshing. And it was a God-given moment, among others, that revealed my own addiction to busyness.

I've lived this kind of margin-less, hectic, barely-finish-one-thing-before-the-next-thing-starts life. It met the American definition of life to the full, one in which more work, more entertainment, and more stuff also means less time and less sleep. More achievements and accolades lead to fewer deep breaths, long meals, and meaningful relationships.

There's a reason why you are flooded with relief when an appointment is cancelled, your boss is out of town, or grandma calls to take the kids. Your days are full to the brim, but something vital is missing.

Considering our daily, weekly, and monthly habits and our national addiction to busyness, it's become quite clear that what's missing in our lives is *SPACE*.

It's something Jesus fought for, and we need it now more than ever.

Making Space

Jesus led a spiritual, theological, and cultural revolution that forever changed the world. He didn't say what was popular. He refused to bow to political correctness. He infuriated the social influencers of his day. He told the recipients of his miracles to keep quiet.

And perhaps most peculiar of all, he regularly fled the scene at the very moment it seemed *least* advantageous to do so. I sometimes wonder how often an exasperated disciple mumbled, "Where's he going *now*?"

Though his leadership was anything but orthodox, it didn't

take long for Jesus' ministry to pick up speed. Mark's Gospel tells us that as soon as Jesus announced, "The kingdom of God has come near," it proved true. In remarkable ways.

We're not even out of the first chapter of Mark's Gospel when a healing extravaganza begins. When Jesus gave the order, the despair of demonic possession and madness of mental illness vacated their friends' bodies and minds. And word of Jesus' power travelled fast.

In this particular scene, the sun had gone down, and Jesus may have been ready for bed, but the people still brought to him all the sick and suffering and traumatized folks they could find.

Before long, the entire town was outside the door—both those who needed miracles and those who just wanted to see one—and Jesus did not disappoint. Mark wrote, "Jesus healed many who had various diseases" and "He also drove out many demons."[1] Many were mended. Many were freed. Many received a brand new life.

Can you picture the scene? I imagine a big tent revival, complete with the miracles of healing and flabbergasted onlookers. Except Jesus is no sweaty charlatan putting on a show. He's the real deal.

And in a surprise turn, in the middle of the life-giving frenzy, at the height of the crowd's wonder and approval, the Miracle Maker exited the building.

He just... disappeared.

He took his leave and did something life-giving for *himself*.

He fought for space.

Read it in the Gospel writer's words:

Very early in the morning, while it was still dark, Jesus got up, left the house and went off to a solitary place where he prayed. [2]

Odds are Jesus didn't sleep a wink that night. It was after sunset when the people brought the broken and bruised and bewitched to Jesus' door.

And he served all of them.

If you scan the rest of the Gospels, paying attention to Jesus' interactions with the poor and lame, sick and possessed, he was in no hurry. He didn't serve microwaved miracles from a buffet line. He looked every person in the eye and gave them his undivided time and attention.

That long night of healings was no different. Yet before dawn, he was up and at 'em. In the midst of very important things, he prioritized the *most* important thing.

He fought for space.

He fought for space to pray. Space to enter the silence. Space to relieve the pressure. Space to be with the Father. Space to remember his name, his calling, his identity.

And if you need proof that making space required a fight, just check out the way his disciples said good morning. Before the sun was up, "Simon and his companions went to look for him... and when they found him, they exclaimed: 'Everyone is looking for you!'"[3]

No doubt. He'd spent the whole night working miracles, completely healing the previously un-helpable. The news spread and Jesus quickly found himself in very high demand.

So what did he do? He slipped away. The pressure was on, but the precedent was set: Jesus would fight for space. He refused to allow his ministry to become manic. And it was his prioritization of space—and, more importantly, what happened in that space—that made his journey possible.

The same is true for you.

A Defined Space

When it comes to a Christian life, space is more than just a gap in your schedule or an obligation-free break from the daily routine. It's more than an empty Saturday. It's more—and better—than simply checking out.

By "space" I mean purposeful time with the Creator. I'm talking about intentional, specific, planned times for silence and reflection. Space to breathe in God's Spirit, stand in awe of the Creator, and listen for Jesus.

This space is often enjoyed in solitude, but it's never spent alone. Space is restorative time with God himself.

For some, that sounds refreshing. For others—maybe you—it already sounds like a daunting list of to-dos.

Impossible, you might say, given your current obligations and desires. *Exhausting,* you might think, given your previous "quiet time" failures.

I get it. But let me assure you of two things:

First, the fight for space is a fight that extinguishes exhaustion, not exacerbates it. It's difficult, but it's worth it. It's challenging, but it's life-changing.

Second, it's not impossible to make this kind of space on a regular basis. Making space is necessary to experience your real life, and before long, you'll wonder how you ever lived without it, or you'll realize you never really did.

In the end, the space you need is the space for which you were designed. And the practice of fighting for space and the practices enjoyed within that space transform from religious to-do lists into spiritual sources of true rest and restoration.

The Point of Space

Jesus' momentary escape in Mark chapter one wasn't a one-off. He had a pattern, a rhythm, a practice of getting away to find and make space. And he invites you into that purpose-filled space with him.

Here's that invitation again, as worded in *The Message*. Jesus said,

> Come to me. Get away with me and you'll recover your life. I'll show you how to take a real rest. Walk with me and work with me —watch how I do it. Learn the unforced rhythms of grace. I won't lay anything heavy or ill-fitting on you. Keep company with me and you'll learn to live freely and lightly. (Matthew 11:28-30 MSG)

The point of fighting for space with Jesus is to get away with him to "recovery your life" and to prepare to walk with him, living "freely and lightly." Our time with God is designed for us to "take a real rest" by experiencing *his* rest.

Different from sleep or just zoning out (both of which are helpful at times), the space that is Rule #1 for a Christian life is centered in relationship with Jesus. This practice is about finding the recovery and readiness that our minds, hearts, and spirits need. It's to him we release our burdens, and it's in him we find the rest we can't live well without.

You and I must fight for space to live a truly Christian life. That space is space with purpose, with a mission, and with amazing results. And believe it or not, you can do it. You can make this kind of space.

Jesus did. And his example is a golden invitation into a new way of being. A way that includes plentiful space.

How to Make Space

In a series of phone and text conversations, an old friend and I delved into the incredible idea that human beings can interact, engage, and converse with God.

My friend struggled to believe it was possible. He asked if I had any insight for experiencing it. I encouraged him to start by carving out space—one hour a week, if possible—to learn to be still, open his mind and heart to God, and learn to listen. His response was telling.

He texted back, "Do you ever think, 'God, you gave me all this stuff to do, and this is the time I have to do it. When am I supposed to ALSO just sit still for an hour??'"

Even the most faith-filled Christians struggle to create space. There are one hundred sixty-eight hours in a week, and my friend was overwhelmed by the idea of setting aside one hour—.6 percent —of his week to the quiet attempt to commune with God.

I don't blame him. We get bombarded by so much in life. But Jesus is slow and quiet, even when everything else in the world— even in our Christian communities—is fast and loud.

In response I texted an honest question: "Are you fulfilled by a life in which you can't find one hour a week to be with him?"

How would *you* answer that question?

Do you feel like you are experiencing the "rich and satisfying" life Jesus promised to give in John 10:10? Or do you have an ache for more? Do you harbor a hunch that there's something better out there and if God is real and what Jesus says is true, then there must be something more—something better—to this Christian life?

Me too. That's what this book is about.

Living a full and satisfying life starts with a commitment to space. You must work hard to push back everything that crowds and cramps. You must learn to slow down, quiet down, and pare down. Once you do, you'll find that God is communicating. And he is communicating *a lot*.

The question is not, will God show up? The question is, will *you and I* show up? And do we have a good plan for doing so?

A Plan: Four Ways to Fight

In his book, *Deep Work,* Cal Newport describes four methods—

the Monastic, Bi-modal, Rhythmic, and Journalistic strategies—for helping professionals make space to focus on and accomplish their most important and valuable work. After reading about deep work, I realized he's on to something.

My aim here is different from Newport's, but his strategies provide a framework that shapes my approach for making space. I renamed his work-based strategies to fit our spiritual goals and incorporated them in the following plan.

I call them Extended, Sabbath, Daily, and Prompted space.

Create any of these four types of space—and engage with God there—and you will begin to discover and live the unparalleled life he designed for you.

Extended Space

As the name implies, extended space is characterized by long periods of solitude and silence. It's for those who are ready and able to carve out weeks, or more, at a time to step away from their busy day-to-day lives to dedicate a long period of time to be with God.

Sabbath Space

Sabbath space is a full day of space interjected regularly into life. Sabbath space is purposeful and uninterrupted, no shorter than eight hours and lasting as long as desired or needed. Afterward, the sabbath space maker returns to the regular routine of life and work.

Daily Space

The most fruitful and easiest ways to fight for space include rhythm or routine. That which we repeat becomes habit, and when it's a powerful habit like forging space, the habit soon bears dynamic fruit. The one who makes daily space creates a rhythm of carving out quiet time to engage with Jesus each day.

Prompted Space

Prompted space is the type you fight for when life's circumstances prompt a need for space with God that is outside your regular routine of sabbath or daily space. It's "as needed" space.

When a sudden setback births painful tears or a long-awaited celebration brings joyful ones, you create prompted space to engage with God. I've made prompted space during and after a crisis and in the wake of one of life's sweetest victories.

Prompted space, like all the other kinds, can be filled with cries and petitions or laughter and praise. Whenever life—or God—prompts a need for space, you make it.

Making Your Space

Which of the above strategies feels natural to you? Which seems challenging but necessary? Which is most realistic in your current stage of life? Or perhaps these types of space don't resonate with you at all, but you're excited to create your own brand of space-making.

There's no one way to do this, and you will likely change your approach depending on your season of life. Few readers are ready and able to block off a month of extended space, but you may be ready to fight for daily space or sabbath space. Or you might feel the need for prompted space.

For me, combining daily space and sabbath space is most fruitful. Most mornings I make space with Jesus for an hour (daily space) to listen, journal my prayers, read Scripture, or work with him on something he specifically asked me to do.

Additionally, I devote the first Friday of each month to Jesus (sabbath space) by setting aside six to eight hours of uninterrupted time to be with him.

The key to it—no matter who you are—is simple: *begin somewhere.* Be it prompted, daily, sabbath, or extended space, make it happen.

With that in mind, let's take a look at the ways Jesus made it happen. We know he fought for space. The question we turn to now is *how.*

How Jesus Fought

The Bible is clear. Making time for quiet, undisturbed space with the Father was a top priority for Jesus. The Gospel writer Luke described it well when he wrote that Jesus "often withdrew to lonely places and prayed."[4]

That's the kind of space we're talking about: quiet solitude to engage with God. As we'll see in the next chapter, these times of space provided Jesus with clarity and purpose for his mission.

While Jesus never articulated a method or framework for pursuing God, Scripture reveals his patterns. You won't be surprised to hear that Jesus employed a variety of strategies to attain this goal.

Let's explore how our Savior fought the fight for space by examining his life in light of these four types of space.

Extended, Sabbath, Daily, and *Prompted Space*

The Gospels tell us that after his baptism, "Jesus, full of the Holy Spirit...was led by the Spirit into the wilderness"[5] for forty days and nights.

It's significant that Jesus' ministry began with a focused, Spirit-filled time of extended space. When you read the accounts for yourself, you'll see it was no stroll in the park. It never is. But the man who changed the world forever began by fighting the good fight for space.

Jesus also prayed all night from time to time: a sabbath approach to space. Luke's Gospel tells us that "Jesus went up on a mountain to pray, and he prayed to God all night."[6] When morning came, Jesus chose the Twelve who became his closest disciples. This time of space helped Jesus prepare for that crucial decision.

In another instance, the Gospel of Matthew says that Jesus "went up into the hills by himself to pray"[7] after a full day of lakeside ministry. Hours later, just before dawn, a squall on the lake interrupted the disciples' commute and Jesus' night of space. In order to walk to them on the water, he had to walk away from another all-night space session.

The Gospels also provide peeks into Jesus' prioritization of daily space. Luke wrote that "Jesus often withdrew to the wilderness for prayer."[8] The operative word is "often." It signals a habit. Jesus frequently stole away to a remote location to listen for the Father's voice.

Later, Luke gives another subtle but significant clue about Jesus' daily pursuit of space. In the terrible hours before Jesus' crucifixion, he invited his compatriots to leave the supper table and join him for prayer. They "left the upstairs room and went as usual to the Mount of Olives."[9]

Two overlooked words unveil Jesus' prayer rhythm. They went "as usual" to the Mount of Olives. Luke helps us see that Jesus fought for space in the best of times and in the worst of times. It was his habit and his harbor in a storm.

Finally, Jesus also fought for prompted space. He incorporated space to prepare for and recover from life's episodes. Check these out.

Matthew tells us that "as soon as Jesus heard the news" that his cousin, John the Baptist, was murdered, he "left in a boat to a remote area to be alone."[10]

After miraculously healing the sick and feeding the five thousand, Jesus "went up into the hills by himself to pray."[11]

And after finishing the Passover meal with his friends, Jesus prepared for his next excruciating task by entering some space for prayer. He took his friends "to a place called Gethsemane, and he said to them, 'Sit here while I go over there to pray.'"[12]

As needed, he broke from the chaos and grind to recover by spending time with his Father. These are prompted strategies for making space if there ever were any.

From day one of Jesus' ministry, there was plenty to do. And the Master could have put the pedal to the metal and raced through all that kingdom activity. But rhythm and space marked his ministry instead of panic and hurry.

Call it extended, sabbath, daily, or prompted space, or use your own terms. Regardless, the witness is clear. At a variety of times, in a variety of ways, and for a variety of reasons, Jesus of Nazareth made space to be with the Father.

You and I are built to do the same.

In the next chapter, we'll explore what happens in your time of space and how to make it fruitful. But for now, the win is just setting aside the time, so let's wrap up this chapter with some helpful ways to start.

How You Can Fight

The tactics for making space are myriad. So, before we jump in, my advice is this: Don't overanalyze the ideas below. Pick the one or two (at most) that fit your personality and ability, or use these ideas as a springboard to design your own.

Whichever you choose, commit to begin fighting for space *this week*. You can do this!

Calendar It

I'll never forget when a woman at my church said, "If I don't put it in my calendar, I'll never pray." That surprised me. I had long admired her life of prayer, but hearing this from her didn't seem... *holy*.

But think about it: All of us live by some sort of schedule. Rather than fight it, *embrace* it. Pick a recurring time and add "SPACE" to your calendar for a minimum of an hour. Resist the urge to think of it as optional.

Once it's in your calendars (including your shared ones), set reminders, and keep the appointment. It will become the most valuable appointment, with the most valuable Person, you have.

So, when is your first "SPACE" appointment?

Get Out of the House

You may need a new (or completely repurposed) space to carve out this new habit.

Perhaps it's a favorite chair in the neighborhood library or bookstore. Maybe, like me, it's an empty church sanctuary. Or maybe it's your porch or a window seat at the new coffee shop. For many, it's the outdoors.

And spiritual stillness doesn't always require physical stillness. I experience some of my most fruitful space during a wandering walk through the woods.

So, where can you go out to allow God to draw you in?

Make Repeat Visits

Because we are people of routine, and our environment contributes to the habits formed there, keeping the same location for space can be helpful. You may eventually have a handful of spots, some inside and some out, where you can lower the brim on life and sink into space with Jesus.

But for starters, pick one spot and try it. Then try it again the next time your "SPACE" notification pops up on your phone.

So, what spot will you revisit, and why?

Power Down

Let me be blunt: Your smart device is a serious devil. The enemy of God uses your smartphone to pull you away from what's good, quiet, and life-giving.

Therefore, a device's power button is one of the best tools you have to fight for space. Remind yourself of its exact location on your phone, tablet, TV, game console, and virtual assistant, and use it regularly. This is crucial for producing space.

So, when do you plan to power down?

––––––––

In Luke 9, Jesus gave his disciples the authority to drive out demons and heal the sick as they ventured out on their first missionary journey. When they failed to cast out the spirit that possessed a boy, he told them, "This kind can come out only by prayer." [13]This is why the disciples asked for a lesson in prayer, not in exorcism.[14]

In the end, what the disciples realized was that Jesus' closeness with the Father fueled his miracle-working power. God equipped and empowered his Son to do the miraculous as Jesus made space to know, connect with, listen to, and surrender to the Father in that space.

The same is true for us. Space is more than a relational break in our chaotic life. It becomes the charging station for our Spirit-led and empowered life.

What Happens When You Don't Fight for Space?

I know from experience that if you don't fight—and fight *hard* —for space with Jesus, life runs you into the ground. Unbearable self-expectations, unachievable cultural demands, and relationship burnout drain our lives. Our uncertainties about life's purpose become arresting anxiety and damning depression.

And all of it leaves us worn out and ruined, wondering about the meaning of it all.

That may sound dramatic, but it's true. The number of people who suffer from isolation and fear, anxiety and depression, mental illness and malnourished relationships is through the roof.[15] The Christian research firm, Barna, reports that "mental health is the new domain of ministry to the next generation."[16] We've got a problem on our hands—one that you may be experiencing personally—worsened by the pace and pressure of everyday life.

If you don't make space to connect with the One in whom your true meaning and identity are sourced, you will never discover them. You will never live them. You will never be satisfied. And you don't want to come to the end of your rope, or the end of this life, and realize you hung your hat and hopes on a cheap substitute for the real One.

That, my dear friend, is what it means to be lost. Lostness is not only about your ultimate destination; it's about your identity and purpose and trajectory *today* as a cherished child of God. And without making space to commune with the One who gives you that identity, you will lose your way.

What Happens When You Do Fight for Space?

I believe that when you fight for space and engage God in it, he will brighten, satisfy, and revive your life.

I'm guessing that two questions have popped into your mind

since you began reading. One is this: Every self-help book on the planet promises to change your life, so what's the difference here?

I'm not talking about weight-loss, productivity, or managing your stock portfolio. I'm talking about a *real, engaged, dynamic,* and *personal* relationship with God. Say what you want about the glories and richness of life in Western civilization, but if there is a God, nothing can compare to *knowing* him.

Your second question might be this: What if I don't want my life to change?

Can I answer honestly? If you didn't want your life to shift toward something better and didn't already believe or hope that life is better as a Jesus follower, you wouldn't have read this far.

A life of following Jesus *is* better. And my bet is that you *do* want your life to change.

The fight for space opens your life, your mind, and even your heart to the possibility and opportunity for engagement with God Almighty. And when that happens, things change.

Your ideas about what's good, true, hopeful, meaningful, and valuable begin to align with what's most true. You experience a kind of calm that's rare in our society and a relationship that's rarer still. You will also receive the energy and focus you need to do the things that deserve your energy and focus.

In very real terms, if you create space and learn to spend it interacting with God, he will mark your life with a sort of vision, depth, wisdom, joy, and relationship that's not possible any other way.

How I Practice Rule #1

At the end of the day, we cannot relate to God without making time to be with him and listen to him. It's the way all relationships work—with other people, and certainly with God.

Here are two practices I first employed to help me begin to fight for space, acclimate to it as a practice, and set it as a priority.

The Daily Pause

A few years back, during a particularly busy season of life, a simple practice called The Daily Pause became a lifeline. Marriage, work, parenting two young children, and a mass of circumstances outside of my control pinned me to the wall. I didn't know how to free up any space again.

Thankfully, I was introduced to The Daily Pause, a refreshingly simple way to make a little space.

The Daily Pause is a sixty-second pause, taken twice a day, to acknowledge God, sense his presence, and refocus your mind and heart on him.

Start by putting an appointment in your calendar as a mandatory meeting or "to-do" item. Title the appointment "SPACE" or "PAUSE," and when your calendar alarm buzzes, stop what you're doing to turn your attention to God. I typically schedule my daily pauses for 10 a.m. and 2 p.m.

The key is this: Set the time and *don't* skip it. But don't beat yourself up if you miss either. Life is crazy. We acknowledged that on the first page of this chapter. The last thing you need is self-inflicted guilt preventing you from trying to fight for space again.

If you make the appointment, commit to it, then give yourself grace and start again when it doesn't happen, you'll be well on your way to a regular rhythm and winning the fight for space.

I borrowed this practice from Christian author, retreat leader, and counselor John Eldredge. He introduces the Daily Pause in his helpful book, *Get Your Life Back,* but his "Pause" app (available for free wherever you download apps) is where the money is. Over time, it can help you develop a simple way to make space and a growing desire to meet with God there.

The beauty of the app is twofold: First, all you have to do is stop, take a deep breath, press play, and Eldredge will lead you through a beautifully simple practice. Second, the app helps you expand your daily pause from sixty seconds to ten minutes slowly over time.

Once you experience the value of short spurts of space, you will begin to fight for longer ones. Remember, whether you use the app or not, the amount of space is not the point: Meeting with God is.

First Fridays

I still remember when a spiritual retreat leader recommended setting aside one full eight-hour day every month to "listen to Jesus." My first thought was, "That's impossible, you moron." But I was so desperate to experience Jesus' rest[17] that I committed to try it.

It's been a true battle, but it has paid huge dividends in my relationship with Jesus, in my understanding of his calling, and in my relationship with my wife and children. What seemed impossible is now necessary. What I once believed I was unable to do, I now know I'm unable to live without.

I set aside six to eight hours the first Friday of every month to listen for, learn from, and enjoy Jesus in the silence of an empty church sanctuary, a walk in the woods, or a bench by the river (or any combination of the three).

Trust me, I understand that this may seem like an impossibility. I did too when the idea was presented to me. Yet now it is a practice I don't live without. It's worth setting as a goal and working hard to achieve it.

———

The Christian life is two steps in, one step out. It's trial and error, hope and frustration, failure and victory. It's what Eugene Peterson titled one of his books: *A Long Obedience in the Same Direction*.

The fight for space is a battle. Developing meaningful, God-filled space takes time and practice. But as you fight—and win—

tangible dividends emerge. But you must keep in mind that space for the sake of space is not the end. It's just the beginning. What you *do* in that space, and with *Whom* you do it, is the real game-changer.

So, what exactly do you do with that hard-won space once you have it? The answer to that question is the very heart and soul of the Christian life, and it's the subject we turn to now in Rule #2.

2

LISTEN TO JESUS

"Listening is the beginning of prayer."
—Mother Teresa

A few years back, my friend Tim said, "Chris, the Christians I know don't need more Bible study. They don't need to go to church more often or do more 'Christian' stuff. What they need is to learn to *listen* to Jesus."

Tim believes we have a relationship problem, not a religion problem. He's so serious about this problem that he's committed his life to remedy it.

Tim and his wife, Kelli, founded and run Seek Well[1], a retreat experience built on the belief that "If we want to live our best life, we need to learn how to be still and listen to Jesus."

Hopefully, after reading the previous chapter, you believe that fighting for space is integral to living a Christian life. But making space for space's sake is not the finish line. The real purpose of making space is so we can *listen to Jesus* in it.

But our hard-fought battles for space are often wasted because most of us were not trained to listen for Jesus.

Now, to be clear, many faithful church leaders teach us to read about Jesus, talk about Jesus, and respect Jesus. Some even teach how to worship Jesus, act like Jesus, and introduce others to Jesus. These are good things for us to learn, and I'm grateful for those who teach us. But there is more to knowing God than respecting and acting like Jesus.

The Scriptures describe devoted followers who *listened* to Jesus. They walked with him and talked with him along life's narrow way, as the old hymn goes.[2] They recognized his voice, received his teaching, asked him questions in true pursuit of the answer, and then they responded to what he said.

My friend's diagnosis about listening to Jesus is spot-on. We can immerse ourselves in Bible study, attend Sunday services weekly, recite prayers ritualistically, and join faith-based justice projects around the globe. But if we don't create space and then listen to Jesus, we can miss the point of life.

The good news is we can learn to listen for, recognize, and understand his voice. We are sheep with a Shepherd, and our Shepherd *speaks*. And the result of learning to listen is a relationship that's the heart and soul of the real life we are made to live.

Why We Listen

The words "lost" and "found" have long been rooted in Christian vernacular. The "lost" are folks not yet reconciled with God through Jesus, while the "found" are those who are. But even the "found" can—and do—lose our way.

We wander. We lose focus. We stop listening.

In this case, being lost is less about eternal separation from God and more about drifting aimlessly through life, missing out on the goodness, fullness, and richness of walking with Jesus day in and day out.

Religion without relationship is no different than secular atheism. Both lead adherents to roam from God, landing them in a narcissistic wasteland. Under the sway of internal voices and external influences we stumble through the desert surviving off the occasional spiritual oasis.

But listening to Jesus turns on the tap and lets the cool water flow. Real life grows[3] as you drink it up.

Jesus said, "My purpose is to give them a rich and satisfying life."[4] For us, that life begins with listening, just as it did for Jesus.

Jesus Listened

Jesus practiced what he preached. Everything he taught his followers to do, he did, including listening to God.

In fact, one of Jesus' best friends portrayed the Messiah as our listening Lord. John's Gospel reminds us repeatedly that Jesus' primary goal was to listen to the Father then to do what he said. He lived his life with no other agenda.

Jesus knows that the most fruitful human life is lived in lockstep with the Father. And like each Rule in this book, Jesus shows us the way.

In John chapter five, Jesus explains,

> I tell you the truth, the Son can do nothing by himself. He does only what he sees the Father doing. Whatever the Father does, the Son also does. For the Father loves the Son and shows him everything he is doing. (John 5:19-20a)

Later Jesus said, "I do nothing on my own initiative, but I speak these things as the Father taught me."[5]

And in a summary statement of his way, Jesus said, "For I have come down from heaven to do the will of God who sent me, not to do my own will."[6]

Jesus constantly listened for the Father's voice and lived his life from what he heard.

If you asked a hundred Christians to describe Jesus' main objective, most would probably say that Jesus came "to die for our sins" or his central task was to "save the lost" or "redeem the world." And these answers are not wrong. Jesus is certainly the Lord and Savior who came to seek and save the lost.[7]

But John's role as a writer seems clear: He was given the task of helping all his readers see that Jesus, the fully human Son of God, wasn't hyper-focused on a pre-scripted game plan. Rather, he tuned all his attention—moment by moment, day by day—on hearing, understanding, and walking with God the Father in real time.

Jesus' sights were set on listening for the Father so he could hear what he needed to hear, know what he needed to know, and ultimately do what he needed to do. He trusted his Father so completely that even in the darkest hour imaginable, he prayed, "I want your will to be done, not mine."[8] And he humbly waited for God's reply.

Jesus listened first, acted second. In so doing, he accomplished all he was born to accomplish, and he teaches us to do the same. Thankfully, our efforts to listen are never futile, because we know and serve a God who still speaks.

Jesus Speaks

John retells a fabulous healing event in chapter nine of his Gospel. Jesus spat in some dirt, rubbed the mud in a blind fellow's eyes, and sent him to wash it out in a pool. The Bible tells us "the man went and washed and came back seeing!"[9]

But despite the miracle, the legalistic religious leaders of the day continued to disbelieve and demonize Jesus.

In an attempt to illuminate their spiritual blindness and annunciate their spiritual deafness, Jesus described a sheep pen, a shepherd, and his sheep. His word picture revealed the truth about salvation, his real identity, and that God's children can hear him and know him.

The Shepherd in the story, who is Jesus, "calls his own sheep by name... and they follow him because they know his voice."[10] Though it took time for his listeners to comprehend the message, Jesus persisted, repeating the goodness of this new Shepherd/sheep paradigm. He concluded his lesson like this:

> I am the good shepherd; I know my own sheep, and they know me, just as my Father knows me and I know the Father. So I sacrifice my life for the sheep. I have other sheep, too, that are not in this sheepfold. I must bring them also. They will listen to my voice, and there will be one flock with one shepherd. (John 10:14-16)

I can't help but wonder what it was like to hear Jesus teach in person. I'm sure it was remarkable.

But here's what I want you to consider: Are Jesus' words pertinent for us today? Do his words about his sheep still resonate, or was his lesson exclusive to the few who walked with him in person through those Galilean hills and valleys?

Many believe Jesus still speaks. Two millennia of Church teaching and experience affirm that even now, an interactive life with him is more than just possible—it's the very nature of being one of his "sheep."

Listening for and hearing Jesus is not some ethereal over-spiritualized wish. It's a distinct reality that's part and parcel of the real Christian life.

In fact, I believe a conversant life with God forms the absolute core of what it means to be Christian. Therefore, learning to listen to Jesus is a vital practice and Rule #2 for living a truly Christian life.

Fight for space.

Listen to Jesus.

Both can be done, and I want to help you learn how. But first, you must make sure it's actually Jesus you're listening for.

Not Exactly Jesus

A few years back I met a young man sitting on our church patio just before the Christmas Eve service began. Let's call him Taylor for now.

When Taylor looked up from his phone, I asked, "Are you going inside?"

"No, man," he replied. "My grandma is in there. She wants me to join her, but I can't bring myself to do it."

"No?" I said. "Why not?"

The honesty of his answer surprised me. He said, "I've prayed for stuff. I've asked God to show up. But if he's real, he's never made himself obvious to me."

Obviously, Taylor was primed for and willing to have a spiritual conversation, so I sat down.

It didn't take long to grasp what he wanted. Taylor wanted God to do exactly what he wanted him to, and in the exact way he wanted him to do it. Taylor believed if God didn't answer his prayers the way he prayed them, God wasn't real.

For example, Taylor asked God to make his girlfriend stay with him. She didn't. So he blamed the breakup on God.

In Taylor's mind, his prayer wasn't answered in the way he wished, so God didn't love him, and, therefore, couldn't be real. Accompanying his grandmother to worship this "God" simply wasn't an option.

Taylor's problem is one we all struggle with from time to time. We unconsciously desire a god who is not the God of the Bible. The god Taylor was looking and listening for was one he'd fashioned in his mind. And that god doesn't exist, and certainly isn't Jesus.

Sometimes we can't pick out the Good Shepherd's voice because, like Taylor, we are listening for someone or something that's not the Good Shepherd at all.

But what does Jesus' voice sound like today? How do we know it's him? And how do we tune in each and every day? I'm excited to say there are several ways. And it all begins with the Bible.

Listening Through the Book

The Gospel of John begins with this remarkable poem:

In the beginning the Word already existed.
　　The Word was with God, and the Word was God.
　　He existed in the beginning with God.
　　God created everything through him, and nothing was created except through him.
　　The Word gave life to everything that was created, and his life brought light to everyone.
　　The light shines in the darkness, and the darkness can never extinguish it. (John 1:1-5)

A few verses later, John revealed who this "Word" is. He wrote,

So the Word became human and made his home among us. He was full of unfailing love and faithfulness. And we have seen his glory, the glory of the Father's one and only Son. (John 1:14)

This poetic opening is about Jesus Christ, and it paints a picture of Jesus as God's Word made flesh. The Creator God who spoke the world into existence through Jesus, became one of us *in* Jesus. And now, the Holy Spirit-inspired written word, Old Testament and New, directs us to Jesus.

It's no wonder then, that the primary source through which we hear Jesus today is the Bible, God's Word. But too few of us have been taught to read it with that in mind.

Most of us learn to read the Bible in the same way we read other nonfiction books: to gather information. We typically read them to master a subject, sharpen a skill, learn about a historical event, or be entertained by someone's life story.

But the problem with reading the Bible that way is that it inverts its true purpose and subverts its true power.

The Bible is unique among books because it's given to *form* us, not inform us. God's text is designed to master *us,* not for us to master it.

God's written Word is the primary way the Holy Spirit speaks, so it's a game-changer when it comes to listening to Jesus. This fact deserves much more exploration, so we'll focus on it next in Rule #3, Read the Bible Slowly. In that chapter, we will see in greater detail how to engage with God through his Word.

Until then, the remainder of this chapter is dedicated to the other ways in which Jesus speaks and how we can listen to him through them.

God's Other Languages

Pastor and author Mark Batterson described how to hear the voice of God in his book *Whisper.* His list of "secondary love languages" (the Bible being the first) lines up with orthodox Christian thought, past and present, and is quite helpful.

In addition to Scripture, Batterson notes, God speaks through desires, doors, dreams, people, promptings, and even pain.[11] To this list I would add peace, believing that God's peace is an integral part of understanding what He's up to.

Here is a description of various ways in which God speaks to us. Prayerfully engage each as you listen, and God will hone the ears of your heart, tuning you into his whisper.

Desire

One of the ways God's Spirit shapes you is through your desires. Psalm 37 says, "Take delight in the Lord, and he will give you the desires of your heart. Commit everything you do to the Lord. Trust him, and he will help you."[12]

Note that the verse says God will *give you your desires,* not that he will give you *what* you desire. The Psalmist teaches that when we delight in God and "commit everything to him," he shapes and orders our desires. And we let him.

This is why Jesus and the Bible are the first and primary ways God speaks. They are the reference point for your longings. If your desires go against either revelation, then your desires aren't given by God.

However, when your desires line up with God's heart as revealed through Jesus and the Bible, pay close attention. Talk about those desires with God. Then listen to what he says and be ready to act.

The sweet spot is when you are so dependent on God and so filled with his Spirit that your desires naturally align with his.

Doors

God's kingdom agenda presses forward, and open doors (new opportunities on the journey) and closed doors (roadblocks and hindrances on the journey) can provide direction as we participate in his restoration project.

That said, every open door or opportunity is not necessarily a God opportunity, and every closed door is not necessarily an ordained obstacle.

In our achievement, accomplishment, and accumulation-based culture, most people advise us to jump at any and every opportunity, particularly if it's one in which we can make more money or "get ahead." But our idols of money, ambition, status, and power incline us to worship some thing or some one other than God (see Rule #10, Name Your Idols). Jesus minced no words on this topic: "No one can serve two masters."[13]

If those idols shape our desires and perspective, they can lead us to take a "golden opportunity" that may be contrary to God's best plan for our lives.

It takes patient, prayerful discernment to know when and how God is using open or closed doors to communicate. But pay attention, because God just might be using them to speak to you.

Dreams

It's undeniable that God spoke in visions and dreams in Scripture. He still does it today. Talk with someone engaged in God's mission in the Middle East and you will likely hear miraculous stories of Jesus speaking to Muslim people through their dreams. And many become followers of *Isa*—Jesus in Arabic—even at the risk of familial, social, economic, and even physical death.

Jesus can and does speak through dreams. If you are open and attentive to this possibility, God might well speak to you this way.

People

That fact that God speaks through people is so apparent that it hardly needs mentioning. If you're involved in a faithful community of other Jesus followers, you've heard Jesus speak through the words of a friend, a prayer, a song, or a preacher. And it's the deep, conscientious, humble spiritual friends who speak God's truth into our lives like no one else.

Friends remind you of the gospel. Friends remind you it's okay to not be okay. Friends call you to repentance when you can't or won't recognize your sinfulness. And friends see God moving in your life in ways you may miss.

God encourages, defends, teaches, questions, pursues, challenges, and loves us through fellow family members of the faith. It's often quite remarkable how clearly God speaks through his community.

Promptings

Different than desires, promptings are nudges—or pulls—from the Holy Spirit. His promptings take time, patience, and focused listening to sort out, and like all the ways God speaks, promptings must be held up against God's Word.

God will not give you a prompting that contradicts his commands, his nature, or the ways of Jesus. They will, however, often contradict what *we* think is prudent or practical in any given moment.

He prompts us to give money when we desire to save, forgive when we want revenge, sacrifice when we want to indulge, and follow when we want to lead. If you're listening, he'll prompt you to speak, listen, give, receive, stop, go, pray, and praise at any given moment on any given day.

Once you're in tune with the way God prompts you, your conversation with him becomes vibrant and immediate as he gives you ample opportunity to grow in obedience and joy.

Pain

There's much theological debate on why God allows pain and suffering. But two things are certain: People experience God's presence in times of pain, and he often communicates loud and clear during our keenest struggles.

Our desperation forces us to reach out to him through prayer, lament, and corporate worship, and we find him reaching back. In our darkest hours we cling to him, and him to us, through the promises of his Word and the proximity and commiseration of his community.

It's often in the midst of agonizing questions like "Why me?" or "How long, Lord?" that God reiterates, "I am here, I have not forgotten you, and I love you." We are most convinced of our need for God and most reliant on his moment-by-moment leadership during hardship. For that reason, pain is grace.

It is counterintuitive, but if you press in toward God rather than running from him during the dark night of the soul, you can experience and hear him in new and powerful ways. He doesn't abandon ship when it seems to be going down. Rather he comes close, communicates, and holds us tight through the long, painful ride.

Peace

God also speaks through a profound sense of peace. This peace —or "settledness" as I like to call it—is confirmation that a desire, dream, doorway, or prompting is a message from him.

God's peace, like his joy, transcends physical circumstances. I've sensed his peace in the brightest moments and in my darkest hours. In both, God's way is confirmed through an internal spiritual peace that defies comprehension.

The Apostle Paul wrote about it this way:

> Don't worry about anything; instead, pray about everything. Tell God what you need, and thank him for all he has done. Then you will experience God's peace, which exceeds anything we can understand. His peace will guard your hearts and minds as you live in Christ Jesus. (Philippians 4:6-7)

That peace, particularly in the throes of trials, is God communicating his will with you.

———

Now that I've described some ways Jesus communicates, let me state two obvious realities. First, most folks aren't used to listening this way. After all, you don't have any friends or relatives who communicate to you through dreams, right?

Your spouse or parents or boss might communicate through verbal promptings on a regular basis, but they can't communicate through your own desires, various open doors, or inner peace. This is God's territory. So, we have to learn to listen in new ways.

Second, it's obvious that God is *not* like you or me. He is altogether different, separate, and *better*. He's multi-faceted. He's mysterious. He is spirit.

He's not hidden, but he's also not human. Why, then, would the way he communicates not be just as unique as he is?

It takes time, practice, patience, and the Spirit's help to learn to listen to Jesus. But your efforts to connect will result in an intimate and conversational relationship like you've never experienced.

Now's the time.

Learn his ways.

Listen every day.

And hold on to your socks.

Because once you're dialed in to your Creator and begin to experience real eternal life, things will never be the same.

What If You Don't Listen to Jesus?

People who face a severe tragedy or live through a life-threatening illness or event often experience a "new lease on life." Many say they didn't feel like they were truly living before the life-changing incident. Their eyes are now opened in a fresh way to the gifts of life.

This is the closest analogy I can find for describing the difference between a Christian who doesn't listen for Jesus and one who does. The one who doesn't know what God says in the Bible, but they have not yet embraced the mysterious but miraculous reality that the Holy Spirit is present and communicates in real time.

To miss that relationship—to go through life only reading about or talking *at* God rather than conversing *with him*—is to experience life halfway, not to the full.

And remember, in the middle of that passage about God's sheep listening to his voice, Jesus says, "My purpose is to give them a rich and satisfying life."[14]

As we listen to the Good Shepherd, we further discover the "rich and satisfying life" he promises. When we don't listen, we experience the other kind of life.

One is full, vibrant, victorious, real. The other is limited, dull, stuck, and illusive.

Which life do you want to live?

What If You Do Listen to Jesus?

When you learn to listen closely, the result is an intimate walk with God himself. If you've been around Christianity a long time, that might seem underwhelming.

Like an astronaut living at the International Space Station, a climber atop Earth's highest peaks, or even a mom and dad of eight living out their dream of parenthood, we can forget just how monumental God's calling is as we live out the daily reality.

Let me remind you, then, that there's no higher and more remarkable experience than knowing the God of the Universe. There *can't* be! And listening to Jesus is the key that opens that very door.

Remember, Jesus said, "I am the good shepherd; I know my own sheep, and they know me, just as my Father knows me and I know the Father."[15]

In the end, God's flock of listening sheep experience and exemplify the unified picture of humanity—the one of God's making in Genesis and remaking in Revelation—*right now*. The joy experienced in belonging, the meaning derived from mission, and the security received from God's protection is ours when we are his sheep who listen to his voice.

Jesus' listeners come to him, follow him, and ultimately find their salvation and true freedom in him. In other words, when we listen to Jesus we experience life—real, full life.[16]

How I Practice Rule #2

The word "practice" has never been more appropriate. Learning to listen requires a lot of it.

Like you, I am still learning to listen to Jesus. And given my deficiencies as a sinful human being, it's something I will continue to learn for the rest of my life.

But that does not overwhelm me. It *excites* me. The more I learn to hear God, the more I want to hear.

Here's how I lean in.

Silence

Silence is a rare commodity these days, but it's vital if you want to understand God. Though he sometimes communicates quite loudly, we most often hear him in a "gentle whisper."[17]

We need times of quiet to connect what we hear through desires, doors, dreams, people, promptings, pain, and peace to the will and direction of God. It takes effort to get used to silence and to learn how to settle our minds when things get quiet, but with practice and patience you can develop the fruitful habit of turning down the volume in life.

Each time I fight for space and listen for Jesus, silence is a key part of the process. Whether it's ten minutes of silence before I begin reading Scripture in the morning, or a full day of silence on a First Friday (see "How I Practice Rule #1), I'm working hard to become accustomed to quiet. I don't want to miss anything the

Master wants to say because my life is constantly filled with noise.

Scripture

The Bible is paramount to my practice. In my times of space (see the "How I Practice" section for Rule #1), I almost always incorporate Scripture. And one of the most fruitful ways I've found to encounter God through his Scripture is devotional reading *and* Bible study.

In devotional reading, the goal is to apply the meaning of Scripture to your life today. The goal of study is to grasp the original meaning and intent of Scripture. The two go hand-in-hand when our aim is to learn God's Word and live according to it.

During my morning times of space, I alternate between these two approaches. For example, at the time of this writing, I am working my way through First and Second Peter with two other books at my side: a journal for use during my devotional reading (see my description of *lectio divina* after Rule #3), and a trustworthy Bible commentary for use during study.

Regardless of which method of reading I choose, I begin with prayer. I never want to forget that hearing from God is his gift, not my doing. So, I ask God to open my heart and mind to him so that I can hear his voice through his written Word. It's a prayer he loves to answer.

Journaling

One of the ways I process my thoughts is through writing. It's also a valuable tool for processing and understanding God's messages to me.

When I write down something I believe God said to me through Scripture, it becomes more concrete. The act of writing helps match my inklings up with Scripture, and I can review them later when I need reminders about what God has said.

———

Listening to Jesus can be challenging. There is a learning curve for all of us. But paying attention to and obeying God is the core of the Christian life.

God promises to communicate, and he promises to richly bless each and every one of us who listens closely and acts on what we hear.[18] Therefore, chief among our tools for living real life is learning to hear, recognize, and respond to his voice.

Thankfully, God makes himself clear. Even if, God forbid, he never again spoke through desires, doors, dreams, people, promptings, pain, or peace, he sent the Word Made Flesh and gave his written Word. And when you slowly read the words of the latter you uncover the message of the former.

It's why Rule #3 is Read the Bible...Slowly, and it's why you'll want to have your Bible close by as you dive into the next Rule. Read on, and listen up.

3

READ THE BIBLE...SLOWLY

"Studying Scripture as much as we can will tune our ear to hear his voice."
—Clare De Graaf

A few years back, I walked across a Christian retreat center parking lot full of cars and church vans. One congregation's mini-bus had these faded words tattooed on the side: *"Read the Bible fast and pray."* I couldn't help but stop and stare, pondering those words for a long moment.

Read the Bible fast and pray.

Something about it wasn't right. You may spot the problem instantly, or you might have to stare at it for a minute or two like I did on that sunny Saturday morning. But go ahead. Take the time. It's worth it. What's missing?

Read the Bible fast and pray.

Some of you saw the problem immediately. But here it is for those who didn't catch it: The church van imperative is missing two commas. And those two commas change everything. Here's how it should have read:

Read the Bible, fast, and pray.

Now it makes sense. Put commas in, and the strange directive to read your Bible as quickly as possible while you pray, transforms into solid encouragement: Engage in the vital Christian disciplines of Bible reading, fasting, and prayer.

Ironically, the incorrect version describes the way many of us approach the Scriptures. We don't regularly fast and pray, but we do, quite regularly, read our Bibles fast.

More Speed, Less Time

In the middle years of the 20th century, futurists around the world predicted that ever-increasing technological advancement would cause humans a problem: boredom. Many believed automation would give us so much free time that we would likely struggle to figure out how to use it all.[1] Sounds like a great problem to have, doesn't it?

I recall this line of thinking reemerging with the advent of email. Communication would become so quick and easy that we would all wrap up our work days a few hours early and our next problem would be deciding which hobbies to pick up.

Does that describe you? Is one of your life's problems that you have too much time on your hands? Somehow I doubt it.

What those folks failed to consider is our insatiable desire for more. To accomplish more. To earn more. To consume more. They also failed to realize that the human being will do almost anything to keep from having to face his own fears, heartaches, and insufficiencies. We do not like looking into the depths of our own souls.

Technology allows us to do more in less time, but we fill every tiny block of unused time with more work, information, or entertainment. Thrilled by—and proud of—our ability to accomplish something, we move directly to the next thing. Some claim to be too driven for free time; most of us are just too distracted.

Day after day, year after year, life is filled with over-active busyness, stressful hustling and posting, and the anxiety-ridden compulsion to do more with less instead of doing less with more. Our days become decades. And all of this trickles down into our lives of faith.

The first three chapters of this book are strategic. The overwhelming and unsustainable cultural demand to keep moving, speed up, do more, live your dreams, and retire young, rich, and happy—and posting it all for the world to see, even though most of the world is too distracted and narcissistic to care—makes us people who don't fight for space, listen to Jesus, or read our Bibles slowly.

We fight to keep up.

We listen to cultural voices.

We read our Bible like we read our email.

And we constantly lose the fight, the voices ruin our hearing, and our consumption of God's Word turns out to be fruitless.

The great question, then, is this: If the pace of our lives produces so little fruit, why do we keep running so fast? Why are we in such a hurry?

Nicholas Carr is the bestselling author of books dissecting the intersections of technology, economics, and culture. His book, *The Shallows: What the Internet is Doing to Our Brains* made him a Pulitzer Prize finalist. His study of the web's impact on our lives and cognitive function is important.

One of Carr's oft-quoted statements is enlightening for our purposes here.

What the Net seems to be doing is chipping away my capacity for concentration and contemplation. Whether I'm online or not, my mind now expects to take in information the way the Net distributes it: in a swiftly moving stream of particles. Once I was a scuba diver in the sea of words. Now I zip along the surface like a guy on a Jet Ski.[2]

Carr's observation of what "the Net" has done to his brain is an astute evaluation of what internet usage does to all our brains. And he wrote that back in 2011.

How much truer is it today?

The web's influence on our brains impacts our time with God. When it comes to reading the Bible, we are high-speed watercraft riders skimming along the surface of eternal truth instead of deep-sea divers into the words, presence, and life of God. When we close the Good Book, we find we are mostly dry instead of being soaked to the bone in the well of God's living water.

Life can be crazy. You may be exhausted by the innumerable daily demands and a vast variety of circumstances that can derail your much-needed and deeply desired stillness with Jesus.

I get it. I'm no different than you.

At the time of this writing, I have two kids under the age of six. Each couple in our circle of friends has between three and six young children. Our lives are a madhouse, and some days a quick skim of Scripture seems to be all we can manage.

A little Bible is better than no Bible, right? Indeed it is. I'll never deny that fact.

But what you will learn, if you have not already, is that speed reading the Scriptures is not how God intended for us to engage with him and his Word. And it will not sustain us for long.

Love it or hate it, God moves at a slower pace than Western society. We must slow down to catch up with him.

We can rush or we can wait. We can run or we can sit. We can skim, or we can dive. If we choose the latter, we can—over time—

develop the patience and practices for delving deep into the Scriptures to breathe in the valuable, life-enhancing, perspective-changing, action-shaping, personally-delivered words of God.

We will get to those practical practices before this chapter is through. But first, it behooves us to recognize the source of our reading problem and the issues it causes before we hit the solutions.

The Word Inside

In the first-century wilderness of Judea, an eccentric prophet named John "The Baptizer" boldly proclaimed God's truth. "Repent of your sins and turn to God, for the kingdom of heaven is near!"[3] John yelled for any and all to hear, "Prepare the way for the Lord's coming!"[4]

Then, one day, it happened. The Lord came. Jesus strode into the Jordan's waters to be baptized, and the onlookers witnessed a miracle.

Matthew recorded it like this:

> After his baptism, as Jesus came up out of the water, the heavens were opened and he saw the Spirit of God descending like a dove and settling on him. And a voice from heaven said, "This is my dearly loved Son, who brings me great joy." (Matthew 3:16-17)

God the Father publicly filled Jesus' love tank then wasted no time commissioning his Son and sending him into the fray to begin his work. "Jesus," Matthew tells us, "was led by the Spirit into the wilderness to be tempted there by the devil."[5]

And it's on his first battlefield that we see Jesus demonstrate why reading the Bible slowly is vital for every child of God.

The Bible tells us he fasted for forty days and nights and "became very hungry."[6] During this terrible physical challenge and profound spiritual excursion, Jesus faced Satan's onslaught.

The devil began his temptation strategy with Jesus' hunger. He attempted to capitalize on Jesus' physical weakness, tempting him with the idol of self-sufficiency: "If you are the son of God, tell these stones to become loaves of bread."[7]

In other words, *Can't you fix your hunger problem? What's the harm in making a little bread for yourself? You are hungry, right? Why wait on your dad when he's obviously not paying you any attention?*

Jesus' response was simple but paramount:

> People do not live by bread alone, but by every word that comes from the mouth of God. (Matthew 4:4)

It would take several books to unpack the theological significance in this single statement. But for now, don't miss what's right on the surface: Jesus fought his enemy with the truth of his Father's Word. His rebuttal is a direct quote of Deuteronomy 8:3.

It's God's Word against the enemy's words. And this is where reading the Bible *slowly* fits into this remarkable scene from our Savior's life.

When we are under duress—when the devil comes to steal, kill, and destroy[8]—it is the truth in God's Word that fights our battle. Therefore it's our ability to remember what he said that will enable us to push back the attack.

Ancient Greek poet Archilochus said, "We don't rise to the level of our expectations; we fall to the level of our training." Trainers and leaders from military boot camps to weekend parenting seminars repeat this quote to emphasize the importance of training.

When things hit the fan, it's our training—that which we've become so familiar with that it's second nature—that pours out of us. Whatever we've internalized rises to the surface, particularly during painful trials.

The truth of Scripture only impacts our lives in the most crucial moments if we have internalized it.[9] We can only internalize it if we've memorized it. And we can only memorize it if we spend time reading it slowly.

Jesus ate the life-giving bread of God's Word. He chewed on it, digested it, internalized it. And at the crucial moment, he had the words he so desperately needed.

People,
Do not live.
By bread alone.
But by every word,
That comes from,
The mouth of God.

There are two important things here. First, note Jesus' intimate familiarity with his Father's words. In a moment of difficult trial, he didn't pull out a scroll. He didn't, it seems, even spend much time thinking.

He could recall the truth he needed at the moment he needed it because he learned it. He was equipped to fight a theological battle with a formidable enemy because he had quick, internal access to the Word of Truth.

It was *in him*. And it came *out* of him. While under duress it *sustained him.*

Second, note that access to God's Word is one thing, but reliance on it is another. Jesus did not just talk the talk. He walked the walk.

In the desert of temptation, the claim that "people do not live by bread alone" was tested and tried. Jesus' provision, his survival, did not come through grit or perseverance or extra layers of body fat. The Son of God survived forty days of no food under a withering desert sun because his sustenance was God himself.

The memorization of Scripture allows us to access it, but the internalization of Scripture allows us to rely on it. And when we rely on the Word of God, we are relying on God himself.

Like the prophets Jeremiah and Ezekiel long before him,[10] Jesus ate the book. And it fed him and formed him. The same will be true for us.

Information vs. Formation

Do you remember learning to read? Early on it was all about proficiency—learning *how* to read. Later in your education, once you could handle the language, you learned *why* we read. Most people read fiction for entertainment or expanding their horizons, and they read non-fiction to acquire knowledge or to master a skill.

All of us—unless you were raised by wolves or taught by a particularly insightful reading teacher—learned to read non-fiction for informational purposes. We read to master something, pass a test, learn a process, or recall a litany of facts.

Each educational setting reinforced this training. Over and over again you learned to open a book and...

- extract the information, not engage with it.
- improve your knowledge, not tend to your soul.
- collect facts, not develop wisdom.
- inform your thinking, not change your life.

We read the facts, acquire the knowledge, implement any needed changes, then move on.

That's how virtually all of us learned to read. And the truth is, for most books, that's just fine. But the Bible is not most books.

Thankfully, halfway through my seminary education, I was given one book to read (which I promptly *skimmed!*) that started to change the way I read the only book that matters.

That remarkable little book was M. Robert Mulholland's, *Shaped By The Word*. I read his words over a decade ago, and I'm *still* chewing on them, letting his insight shape the way I approach reading the Word of God.

Mulholland explained two ways of reading the Bible's text: We can read to be informed or read to be *formed*. "In informational reading," he wrote, "we seek to grasp the control, to master the text."

In contrast, he argued, the point of *formational* reading is "to allow the text to master you. In reading the Bible this means we come to the text with an openness to hear, to receive, to respond, to be a servant of the Word rather than a master of the text."[11]

Reading for formation changes everything. I wrote it this way in the last chapter: The Bible is unique among books because it's given to *form* us, not inform us. The text is designed to master *us,* not for us to master it.

The Bible itself puts it this way:

> For the word of God is alive and powerful. It is sharper than the sharpest two-edged sword, cutting between soul and spirit, between joint and marrow. It exposes our innermost thoughts and desires. (Hebrews 4:12)

What other book have you read that's *alive?* We've all read meaningful, helpful, and inspiring books. But what other book have you read that was reading *you,* piercing your innermost soul and spirit and laying bare your ideas, dreams, and cravings?

Paul wrote a letter to his gospel protégé, Timothy. In it he said,

> All Scripture is inspired by God and is useful to teach us what is true and to make us realize what is wrong in our lives. It corrects us when we are wrong and teaches us to do what is right. God uses it to prepare and equip his people to do every good work. (2 Timothy 3:16-17)

In short, God's Word—Jesus the Word made flesh[12] and the Bible's testimony about God and humanity—is the primary way that God speaks. It's not the only, but it's the foremost way he has, does, and will communicate to those with ears to hear and the discipline to go slow.

Rethink This Book

There are two more principles to discuss that will help us slow down and relish God's book. We need to rethink what kind of book it is and why we are consuming it. Both are crucial for our proper digestion of this God-given feast.

First, let's tackle what kind of book the Bible is.

The Bible is the true story of God and humanity, from the first light of creation to the final culmination of history. It's the remarkable revelation of who God is, who we are, why the world was made, what went wrong, and what God has done and will do to redeem every broken thing.

However, many readers approach the Bible as if it were something far less remarkable: a moral guidebook or a history lesson. Even if they believe it's the divinely inspired Word of God, they still approach it the way they've been taught to approach other books. They read it to learn God's instructions for living or to grasp religious history, or some combination of both.

Unfortunately, both approaches miss the mark.

The Bible is designed to do more (far more!) than provide a code of conduct or a history lesson. The Bible intends to introduce you to the God of the universe. And the introduction is personal, not informational.

Entertainment magazines and websites "introduce" us to celebrities all the time by publishing the facts and events of their lives. But if you knock on your favorite movie star's door, you won't be treated like an old pal. You'll earn a visit to the local police station instead.

What you read about the rich and famous gives a pile of information, but it never provides a personal introduction.

Far too many of us read the Bible as if its authors wrote a timeless entertainment rag about the ultimate celebrity. We collect fun, freaky, and fascinating facts about God, but we don't *know* him.

The Bible, thankfully, is *way* better than that. It's the true story of God and humanity and the divine invitation to receive God's love, to be forgiven and redeemed, and to know him now and forever.

As you sit with the words in his text, you sit with him. When you take it slowly, you take him seriously. When you meditate on his Word, when you listen for him to speak through it, when you memorize and internalize it, you interact with him in ways that make your relationship real and strong, vibrant and immediate.

Rethinking God's book opens you to experience the God behind the book in ever more real and dynamic ways.

Begin With Why

Not only do you need to rethink what kind of book the Bible is, you might also need to rethink why you are reading it.

Most booksellers file the Bible under "Christianity" or "Religion." But given the way many of us read this ancient text you would think it belongs in the self-help section.

We're duped by our narcissistic age, and we read God's Word as if it was primarily about us. We read the ancient stories and interpret the timeless truth through an egocentric lens that twists its intended purpose and thwarts our efforts to understand God's mission for us.

So here is a truth I need you to grasp. Highlight it. Write it down. Memorize it right now.

The Bible is *not* about you.

The Bible is *for* you, but it's not *about* you. That may seem like a subtle, technical difference, but it's a vital one that changes the way you read and understand God's Word.

The reason we must learn to read the Bible slowly is precisely because it's not a repository of quick-fix solutions to all of life's problems. Rather, we read it slowly to engage in a conversation with the living God of the universe. *He* is the One the book is all about, after all.

In our reading and reflecting, meditating and memorizing, we come to him with our broken, confused, disordered, and altogether frustrating lives so we can be changed. We come to be made whole in our heart, soul, and mind.

Now that might sound like the ultimate self-help book, but let me repeat the key: This grand book, the greatest ever written, is not about you. The Book is all about Jesus, God's presence among us, and his creation, redemption, and restoration of all things. Of which you get to partake and enjoy.

So why read the Bible? To "take hold of the life that is truly life."[13] And why read it slowly? To engage with God's Spirit personally and make sure we don't blow right past anything he wants to communicate.

We read the Bible slowly so we can understand God, learn his will for the world, find our place in his story, and then spend the remainder of our lives living real life.

That's the *why*, friends. Let's now turn our attention to the *how*.

Reading for All It's Worth

The Bible is an ever-fresh message from God. It's nothing short of miraculous. Here's how you settle into its pages to listen to Jesus.

You read the Bible intentionally, prayerfully, and corporately.

Intentionally

Some of us grew up in church on a steady diet of the Bible's most famous and fascinating stories. We were intrigued by two naked humans in a garden, wild animals marching onto an ark, a scrawny kid slaying a giant, and—of course—a man who gives vision to the blind, turns snacks into feasts, and came back to life after his gruesome murder.

But recalling the children's version of those stories is not the same as interacting with God in Scripture now.

Reading the Bible intentionally means reading with the desire and plan to engage rather than be entertained, to be formed rather than informed, to allow God to reach us rather than just teach us. Intentional reading is purposeful.

Far too many of us—myself included—learned to read the Scriptures out of duty. We read intentionally but for all the wrong reasons. We read because it's what "good" Christians do.

But true intentionality is when we read for the reasons *God* wants. God wants us to read his Word because we can find him there. God told his people through the prophet Jeremiah, "If you look for me wholeheartedly, you will find me."[14]

Prayerfully

The single greatest "tip" for engaging God through Scripture is to read the Bible prayerfully. That means to read God's Word as *part* of your prayer conversation with him, not separately. I recommend three aspects of this practice: Ask God, Go Slow, and Respond Truthfully.

1. *Ask God* - Do you ask God to illuminate his Word for you each time you begin to read it? It's a simple but powerful request. When you make it, you recognize God's presence, invite him to act, and prepare to experience his power.

The cliche is true: God is a gentleman. He's not interested in forcing himself into your Bible reading time. A simple prayer of longing for God to show up and communicate to you through his Word will set the stage for him to speak.

2. *Go Slow* - Ever done a year-long Bible-reading plan? It's tough, and it's the opposite of slow. The benefit of plowing through

all of Scripture in three hundred sixty-five days is the sweeping view of God's true story it provides. And it has its place—to understand the parts we must know the whole.

But typically, God moves at a different pace than we do, and reading the Bible for formation requires slowing down. *Way* down.

Ask God to enliven, empower, and interrupt your reading. Then tell him you are listening, and ask him to speak.

Then choose a small chunk of Scripture to focus on. Maybe you sense God's tug toward a particular chapter or section. (If so, you're listening already!)

I recommend starting with five to ten verses, no more than a chapter, in a Gospel or the Psalms. Finally, read that text, and read it *slowly.*

Did you grasp what was going on? Did you get a general idea of the pace, the event, the instruction, the prayer, the big idea? Good.

Now read it again.

Notice the nuances and wrestle with the words. As you read, ask God what he wants you to see. Then pay close attention.

He might highlight a specific word or phrase or even a fully formed idea for you to meditate on.

He might convict you of sin so you can confess, receive his forgiveness, and repent.

He might bring to mind a name—someone with whom he wants you to relate in a new, different, or better way.

He might have you rest in the silence to accept his presence, warm to his slow pace, and enjoy him before the madness of another day begins.

3. *Respond Truthfully* - The third way to read prayerfully is to respond honestly to what God says *as you read.* Responding in real time develops your ability to engage with him and turns a reading session into a conversation. Highlight the verse, jot a note in the margin, or write out all your God-fueled thoughts in a journal.

And *keep listening.*

God raised the ideas, convictions, or questions, and now he

wants to talk with you about them. Meditate on his words, read the passage again, allow God to cement his Truth within you.

One more key thought: Jesus told the woman at the well that God looks for those who worship him in spirit and in truth.[15] If your truthful response is a question, skepticism, or uncertainty, don't be afraid to voice it. Write out your thoughts and ask God to give you his.

God is not bothered by our questions, and we should never be afraid of them. After all, what better way to converse than to ask? And be ready, because God will use his text to provide answers and ask you some questions, too.

Corporately

Learning to understand what God says requires regular engagement with his Word in two essential ways: individually—via your personal forms of Bible reading, meditating, and study—and corporately—with a group of people with whom you can explore the mystery and beauty of God's words.

It's easy to overlook the latter. While it's crucial that we pursue individual times of quiet with God's Word, it's equally vital that we read it with others. We'll talk about this more in Rule #5, Join the Church.

Until then, it's sufficient to say that God's work in you is personal, but it's not private. You are designed to know and hear God better as you engage with him alongside others.

What If You Don't Read the Bible Slowly?

I don't want to overstate it, but if you don't read your Bible slowly, you can miss God altogether.

The whole point of Christianity is to be reunited with the God of the universe. He made us, loves us, and wants us to experience the life he built us for. So "missing" God himself is missing out on everything life was designed to be.

Now we must be intellectually honest. Reading the Bible quickly is better than not reading it at all. But reading it fast, or purely as a source of religious information, reduces your ability to engage with God. When you read it too quickly—or fail to read it at all—you hamper your ability to understand, relate to, and interact with God.

The ramifications of that are deep and wide. Many live with God in mind, but he makes little impact in their lives. Because they breeze through the Bible as religious reading instead of a doorway to the Divine, they are unaware of spiritual realities, can't battle spiritual evil, and belong to the royal family of God in name only. They don't have—and can't foster—a dynamic and personal relationship with him.

Human beings need *transformation*, not only information. We cannot live the human life without being shaped, sharpened, and shifted from who we tend to be to who we were made to be. And reading the Bible for information only—or reading the Bible quickly and piecemeal—prevents that from happening.

The only hope we have for transformation is engagement with God, and he has given his Word and his Spirit for that purpose. But we cannot engage fully with one and not the other. And disengagement from God renders you impotent against the evil of the world, useless in helping others thrive, and living a banal human existence instead of a fully alive one.

What If You Do Read the Bible Slowly?

Imagine reaching the ripe old age of ninety and someone showed you a film of the most fulfilled, purposeful, aware, and alive version of your life. Then, imagine they showed a film version of your *actual* life.

Would they match? Would they be consistent in vibrancy,

openness, curiosity, courage, and joy—even if your life was quite difficult?

Or would the two films be different? And if so, wouldn't you want to know how you could have lived the version that was one hundred percent alive?

The answer is through personal engagement with God himself. He is the Author and Perfector of our faith, the Creator and core of true human life. Reading the Bible slowly, internalizing its truth about God, and allowing him to form us through it is one of the central ways we live this portion of eternal life fully engaged, fully awake, fully alive.

Reading the Bible quickly—or just for information—means you will miss a lot. Not just words on a page, but breath in our lungs.

Slow down, and life fills up.

Speed up, and life runs out.

Add this kind of Bible reading to prayer, community life, service, repentance, and worship, and you move from living a fractured existence to living the full, complete, and dynamic human life God designed you for.

How I Practice Rule #3

If you long to slow down your Bible reading to listen for Jesus, *lectio divina* is a helpful and dynamic practice. I practice *lectio divina* personally and when I lead groups in prayer. I mentioned it briefly in Rule #2, but here's a more detailed explanation.

Lectio divina—or divine reading—is the ancient practice of slowly and repeatedly reading a short passage of Scripture with extended moments of silence between each reading. The two minutes (or more) of silence between readings provides space for you to listen for specific words or phrases from the Scripture. God may then make connections between his Word and the circumstances in your life and in our world.

In this way, reading becomes more than reading: it becomes prayer. It becomes listening to Jesus.

Some of the most fruitful mornings I have with God are facilitated by a *lectio divina* style reading. I soak in the Scripture, sit in the stillness, and enjoy God's presence in Spirit and in truth.

Here's a step-by-step breakdown for your own time of divine reading:

Step 1: Choose a passage of Scripture between two and ten verses long. Psalm 1, 3, and 23, Isaiah 30:15-21, Matthew 11:28-30, Mark 1:9-15, Luke 5:4-11, and John 15:1-8 or 9-17 are great places to start.

Step 2: Take three to five minutes of silence to breathe deeply and settle your heart and mind. Focus your attention on God. Three minutes of silence will feel like *forever* at first. But worry not —with practice you will learn to settle in and become comfortable in the quiet.

Step 3: Read the passage slowly, out loud. As you read, listen for any word or phrase that catches your attention in particular. Then during the silence, meditate on that single word or phrase.

Step 4: Read the passage slowly for the second time, again listening for God to highlight a single word or phrase. It may be the same word or phrase or a different one.

In the silence after this reading, let the word "roll around" in your mind. Listen to it. Ruminate on it. Ask God to help you keep it and remember it.

Step 5: Read the passage a third time. In the two minutes of silence that follow, ask God the question, *How does this word or phrase connect with my life today?*

Pay close attention to how God connects the dots. If you sense a connection, meditate on it. If not, that's okay too. Enjoy the silence, and stay open to the Lord.

Step 6: For the final time, read the passage slowly then enter two more minutes of silence. This time, read and listen with this question in mind: *Lord, do you have a gift, an invitation, or a specific direction for me today?*

Pay close attention in the silence for God to offer one or the other. If you sense him speaking, respond.

Step 7: Stay in silence with Jesus for a few last minutes or for as long as you like. Receive his love for you. Thank him. Worship him. Enjoy him. Respond honestly to the Lord based on your experience.

Step 8: Write down the word or phrase, the connection to your life, and any invitation, gift, or direction God gave. Journaling helps cement this moment in your mind and heart, and later you can return to it to be reminded of what Jesus said.

———

The Christian who fights for space—then dedicates that space to listening to Jesus by reading the Bible slowly—soon realizes that there is more to life than what meets the eye. God's Word comes alive, Jesus' presence is realized, and a deep, almost unexplainable thirst for more is born.

That thirst is not easily quenched in a society hell-bent on knocking God off his pedestal. But if you long to live your real life —to experience the depth and power and pure aliveness that God intends for you—there is good news.

God offers far more than the paradigms of this broken and limited world. He offers us every mysterious and miraculous part of himself. And that's what Rule #4 is all about.

4

BECOME A MYSTIC

"We are not human beings having spiritual experiences. We are spiritual beings having human experiences."
—Pierre Teilhard de Chardin

Life in the post-Enlightenment West is remarkable. Western societies are the richest, most comfortable, and most free societies on Earth.

Besides paving the way for the revolutions in science and technology that make our lifestyle, wealth, and education possible, Enlightenment thought shifted the way we see reality. Western humanity pulled its trust from the spiritual and invisible and placed it in the physical and measurable. The prevailing ideology that resulted is rationalism.

Ultimately, centuries later, the rationalistic Western world places its hope and trust in the power of the human intellect. It's by the power of reason, the thought goes, that human beings will solve all human problems. Eventually, the disciplines of science, education, sociology, and good ole' hard work will remedy our woes, guarantee human thriving, and build utopia.

Yet even with rationalism's four hundred year runway, the utopia plane is far from taking flight.

Rational Blindness

Unfortunately, rationalistic thought leaves no room for spiritual realities—nothing mystical, mysterious, or miraculous—because it can't understand things of the spirit. It has no tools to. It's a full commitment to human reason, and the scientific method limits true human experience to only what can be measured through the physical senses and scientific experimentation and reproduction.

Rationalism reduces the human being to a mass of measured biology, a product of chance and evolution, an incredible biological machine that can, in time, be comprehensively rationalized and measured and diagnosed.

We don't dwell on this in our daily lives, but if you pull a fine-toothed rationalism comb through your life experience, you will find that this way of thinking is pervasive.

Your education is based on rationalism. Your health care is scientific. Even what you deem to be common sense is so perfectly tuned to rationalism that anything outside of what's measurable and repeatable goes in the "unexplained" or "irrational" pile. You are tempted to dismiss and forget it without ever exploring or engaging it.

We are far more comfortable with what seems rational, observable, and measurable.

Yet there remains that nagging feeling that there's more to life than this. There's an ache in our soul we can't explain away. And because many of us have personal experiences that don't fit in measured, rational boxes, rationalism leaves us stranded with fewer answers, not more. It may help explain the "whats" and "hows" of human life, but rationalism is useless in our pursuit of the "who" and "why" behind human life.

Emotional Loneliness

Rationalism shaped the Western world into the phenomenon it is today. But the 21st century has introduced a new challenger that wages war against rationalism. This new mode of operating is called emotionalism, and it is a formidable foe.

Emotionalism can be defined as being ruled, almost in total, by one's own feelings and emotions. It's a state of being in which individuals speak, act, and think based entirely on the way they feel.

In emotionalism, facts don't matter. There's no objective reality. Feelings rule the day and everything is subjective, including truth itself. What an individual *feels* is true is deemed true.

The unintended consequence of individualism (freedom for individuals to make their own decisions without being controlled by the state or a collective group), is egocentrism (the inability to accurately assume or understand any perspective other than one's own). Egocentrism is the evil twin of individualism.

Freedom to think and act for oneself has turned into the *inability* to think or act on behalf of anyone else. And when you are no longer accountable to the greater group, society, or family of which you are a part, emotionalism is the natural result.

Across a wide spectrum—from theology to family, politics to medicine, sports to education—the world is being forced to acquiesce and align itself with all the particular, emotional "truths" of a mass of individuals rather than holding the mass of individuals to an objective reality that's true for everyone.

It's no exaggeration to say emotionalism will destroy ordered society. It has the potential to end objective thought and even the rule of law. After all, if individual human beings are the arbiters of truth based on their own feelings, what stops them from doing *anything* they feel like doing, and who will be able to say they are wrong?

Because this new age of emotionalism leaves no room for an objective truth, it has no room for an objective Truth-Giver. Emotionalism leads us to believe all of life is subject to one's inner workings with little consideration for how screwed up those inner workings are. It eliminates the possibility of an objective truth or reality for all people. It's the origin of chaos.

The more individualistic and egocentric we become, the more destructive we are to society. Why? Because in the end, families, societies, and the global community we now live in can't function if it's every-man-for-himself. Like it or not, we are all connected, and a society full of individuals doing what each believes is good for only himself will not function well for long.

———

A society built on rationalism or emotionalism leaves no room for God. Both deny his existence. Rationalism relies wholly on the power of human intellect to shape and influence the world while emotionalism relies wholly on feelings to rule and direct an individual's life.

Where, then, is God's place in these two worldviews? He has none. And his absence is deeply felt.

Rationalism eliminates true spirituality and disconnects us from true human experience. Emotionalism eliminates true community and leaves us all alone.

That's the bad news. Here's the good news: There *is* a better option. Become a Christian mystic.

Press into the spiritual reality of the world and its Creator and the door to becoming truly human will fly open. You will become an active member of a universal God-centered family, and you will never be alone again.

Who Is He?

Jesus was neither a "rationalist" nor an "emotionalist." He was a mystic. He believed spiritual truth and reality are more expansive than the intellect, and unity with God through self-surrender is where true human life is lived.

Jesus was unified with God his Father and his life was replete with miracles. The Gospels are chock full of their retellings.

After one such miracle—the giving of sight to a blind man— Jesus posed an important question to his band of brothers. He asked, "Who do people say I am?" They replied, "some say John the Baptist, some say Elijah, and others say you are one of the other prophets."[1] But when Jesus asked who *they* thought he was, Peter hit the nail on the head: "You are the Messiah."[2]

Peter identified Jesus' job title but struggled with Jesus' job description. Though Jesus explained that the religious establishment would have him tortured and murdered, Peter and the crew resisted the idea that Messiah was a suffering servant.[3] They were confused about who Jesus really was and what he came to do.

So, Jesus took his closest friends—Peter, James, and John—out for some alone time and a mountain-top experience that provided another piece to the identity puzzle.

Jesus, as it turns out, was no run-of-the-mill military leader or king. He wasn't Moses, Elijah, or any other back-from-the-brink prophet.

He was the very Son of God.

Mystic Mountain

Together they climbed a high mountain, and at its pinnacle something remarkable—something *mystical*—happened.

As the men watched, Jesus' appearance was transformed, and his clothes became dazzling white, far whiter than any earthly bleach could ever make them. Then Elijah and Moses appeared and began talking with Jesus. (Mark 9:2-4)

Trippy, right? Imagine following your closest friend up a mountain on a weekend getaway only to have something like *this* happen. It would fall in one of two categories: altitude-induced hallucination or a true miracle moment.

The side-by-side appearance of Moses and Elijah proved to them that Jesus was different from what others speculated. He was no recycled prophet. He was the one and only Son of the living God.

The Bible tells us,

Then a cloud overshadowed them, and a voice from the cloud said, "This is my dearly loved Son. Listen to him." Suddenly, when they looked around, Moses and Elijah were gone, and they saw only Jesus with them. (Mark 9:7-8)

The voice of God declared that this was his beloved son, set apart from God's prophets before him, and thus he was the One to most closely listen to and follow.

Though it did not answer all their questions, the experience afforded Jesus' closest friends a deeper understanding of this mysterious Messiah. And if Peter's New Testament letters are any indication, that experience sustained him in God's mission for decades.[4]

They had seen Jesus' physical miracles. But they needed a mystical experience with God himself to open their eyes to his one true way.

We need the same. And God's miraculous way is active all around us if we will but allow him to take us up the mountain and open our eyes to who this Jesus is and what's possible through him.

Christian Mystics

I once served as an associate pastor at a church in Southern California. One Sunday, our lead pastor preached from Scripture about the mysterious, mystical, and miraculous Spirit of God.

After the service one congregant shook his hand and smirked, "You're not becoming a mystic now, are you?" Our pastor smiled, kept shaking his hand, and said, "Every Christian is a mystic, my friend. Every one."

His response shocked the congregant, but it was true. And I, for one, was grateful that the man leading our church was unafraid—particularly in this theologically conservative congregation—to declare that this thing we are doing, the turning our lives over to God himself in Jesus Christ, is a mystical and miraculous thing. There's no way around it.

A dictionary defines the word "mystic" as "a person who seeks by contemplation and self-surrender to obtain unity with or absorption into the Deity or the absolute, or who believes in the spiritual apprehension of truths that are beyond the intellect."

The greatest mystery and miracle of the Christian faith, to me, is not salvation from sin, God's sovereignty and omniscience, or even life after death. The greatest mystery and miracle is the opportunity to become a true member of God's family and be *unified with God himself.*

In John 17, Jesus prays a remarkable prayer. I encourage you to spend time reading and reflecting on each verse of it, *lectio divina*-style. But for our purposes here, let's focus in on what Jesus prayed starting in verse 20.

> I am praying not only for these disciples but also for all who will ever believe in me through their message. I pray that they will all be one, just as you and I are one—as you are in me, Father, and I am in you. *And may they be in us* so that the world will believe you sent me.

I have given them the glory you gave me, so they may be one as we are one. *I am in them and you are in me.* May they experience such perfect unity that the world will know that you sent me and that you love them as much as you love me...I have revealed you to them, and I will continue to do so. Then your love for me will be in them, and *I will be in them.* (John 17:20-23, 26)

I italicized some key words so you wouldn't miss them. God in the flesh, Jesus, spoke with God the Father, and prayed that by the Spirit we would all be united to him and with one another. Take a moment to think about that.

Why would Jesus pray it if it wasn't possible? And how can we miss the undeniably mystical nature of this prayer? The very possibility of this kind of unity with God is mind-blowing.

And Jesus' prayer request is not a one-off. Consider these Scriptures:

When I am raised to life again, you will know that I am in my Father, and you are in me, and I am in you. (John 14:20)

Remain in me, and I will remain in you. For a branch cannot produce fruit if it is severed from the vine, and you cannot be fruitful unless you remain in me. Yes, I am the vine; you are the branches. Those who remain in me, and I in them, will produce much fruit. For apart from me you can do nothing. (John 15:4-5)

Don't you realize that all of you together are the temple of God and that the Spirit of God lives in you? God will destroy anyone who destroys this temple. For God's temple is holy, and you are that temple. (1 Corinthians 3:16)

The person who is joined to the Lord is one spirit with him. (1 Corinthians 6:17)

What remarkable realities these verses point to. What mystical means. What beautiful opportunities.

Christian preachers, leaders, book writers, and everyday believers talk much about following God, being saved by Jesus, serving those in need, and participating in God's church.

But this—*this* is where it all begins: the mysterious, miraculous, and mystical opportunity to be joined with God, filled by the Holy Spirit, and become his adopted son or daughter through faith in Jesus Christ.

It is this mystical reality that makes all the other miracles of the Christian life possible. But if you don't open your heart to the spiritual reality of God—if you don't become a mystic—you will miss every miracle on the list.

The Miracle that Started It All

Many Christians behave and pray as if they don't really believe in miracles, and some come right out and say it. Like the man in conversation with my former pastor, they are skeptical about the mystical.

To be frank, I find their disbelief strange. After all, isn't the entire Christian faith predicated on a miracle? In his letter to Jesus followers in a city called Corinth, the Apostle Paul wrote this interesting bit:

> But tell me this—since we preach that Christ rose from the dead, why are some of you saying there will be no resurrection of the dead? For if there is no resurrection of the dead, then Christ has not been raised either. And if Christ has not been raised, then all our preaching is useless, and your faith is useless.
>
> And we apostles would all be lying about God—for we have said that God raised Christ from the grave. But that can't be true if there is no resurrection of the dead. And if there is no resurrec-

tion of the dead, then Christ has not been raised. And if Christ has not been raised, then your faith is useless and you are still guilty of your sins.

In that case, all who have died believing in Christ are lost! And if our hope in Christ is only for this life, we are more to be pitied than anyone in the world. But in fact, Christ has been raised from the dead. He is the first of a great harvest of all who have died. (1 Corinthians 15:12-20)

Christians base our entire belief system on one single historical miracle: the resurrection from the dead of Jesus of Nazareth. If Jesus never died and rose from the grave, we Christians are fools.

As Paul asserted, our theology is a sham, our beliefs are empty, and our devotion is a joke if it didn't happen. And if it's a lie, we ought to at least have the intellectual honesty and self-respect to stop preaching it as truth and just close up shop.

But, if it *is* true—as the first eyewitnesses attested to and history affirms—then it's a miracle that changes everything. *Everything.*

Everyday Miracles

The resurrection of Jesus is the primary miracle and the linchpin of Christianity, but it's not the only miracle integral to the Christian story and experience. And by God's goodness, his miracles are clearly recorded in the pages of Scripture, *and* they still happen today.

Besides Jesus' resurrection, the Bible is full of miracles. From the beginning—when God spoke the world into existence in Genesis 1—to the end—when Jesus gave John a divine vision of the future in Revelation—God's book is full of his miraculous work.

Let's focus now on some of the less-obvious miracles; the mystical and miraculous experiences of the everyday Christian life.

The Presence: God With Us

Immanuel is a biblical name for Jesus which literally means "God with us." But I once heard a preacher say that the entire Bible can be summarized with those three words.[5] That's because Scripture's story of God and humanity is all about God being with us. Grab a Bible and you'll see.

Hans Christian Andersen once said, "The whole world is a series of miracles... but we're so used to them that we call them ordinary things."[6] I think this is particularly true regarding God's presence.

There's a reason why mature Christians tout a "relationship" with God. It's because he's close. He's intimate. He's personal. He handcrafted the world you inhabit, and he's quite fond of you, so he stays close by. And that's miracle number one of the Christian experience.

The Word: God Speaks

The second thing you will notice if you skim the Bible is that God is not silent. It's difficult to read any chapter from Genesis to Revelation without the author noting that "God said" something. That phrase—or one like it—appears hundreds of times in the text. Like his presence, God's speech is so ubiquitous in the pages that it no longer seems miraculous. But it is. And it *still* happens.

As we covered in Rule #2, God continues to communicate—to people and persons, corporately and individually. And Rule #3 was all about God's primary mode of communication, the Bible.

This miraculous book is more than a source of information; it's one of God's tools for transformation. By it we receive a clear picture of who God is, who we are, and what God is doing in and through his Creation. On top of that, the Spirit of God uses his word to mold and make us.

God communicates, and it's a mystical and mysterious part of who he is and how he operates that never ceases to amaze.

Prayer: God Listens

I'm not sure which is more miraculous: that God speaks, or God listens. The more I chew on it, the more I'm inclined to say the latter.

After all, *we* are the created ones, so what business do we have speaking to the Creator? It's easy for me to imagine a deity that dictates directives to his minions, but it's shocking that our great God is humble and kind enough to listen to his creatures.

We have no inherent right to approach him—a being so holy and heavenly, so awesome and other, so big and so beautiful. But thankfully, and miraculously, we are given the privilege.

Put these two truths together—God speaks *and* God listens—and you end up with the most miraculous thing of all: God is conversational. He talks, can be talked to, and talked with. Hopefully you're growing to see that God is in the miracle business, and communicating with his Creation is par for the miraculous course.

The Body of Christ: God Indwells

The family of God, the Church, is referred to as the Body of Christ in the New Testament[7] because Jesus promised to dwell in us, individually and corporately.[8] And he didn't mean it in some esoteric symbolic way. He means to dwell, literally, by his Spirit, within his people.

Think about what a distinct miracle this is. We, God's Church, are a ragtag group of misfits whose only distinction from everyone else in the world is that we've surrendered to God through Jesus, and the Holy Spirit dwells in us.

We realize we are too bent and broken to be fruitful on our own.[9] But because of Jesus in us, we become united, humble, and generous. Because of Jesus in us, the poor are fed, the lonely are befriended, and the sick are tended and healed. Because of Jesus in us, children are taught and protected, marriages last and thrive, parents and the elderly are honored, and neighborhoods become communities.

When we pray "your kingdom come, your will be done on earth as it is in heaven,"[10] Jesus answers, "yes." He fills us with himself—he indwells us—then tells us to get to work, participating in his kingdom as a submitted, surrendered, and joyfully obedient crew. It's miracle upon miracle, if you ask me.

Transformation: God Changes Us

Nothing transforms a human being like God. No self-help book, no workout, no surgery, and no amount of willpower can do the soul-shaping work that God does.

When you trust Jesus Christ by faith, receive his Spirit into your life, and live by the Word that comes from the mouth of God, the Holy Spirit molds you, makes you, and moves you. He feeds you, fills you, and frees you. You become a new creation.[11] And that's a miracle of God.

Love: God Is

If you've ever encountered true love—for someone else or from someone else—you know it's not quantifiable. It's mysterious. Beautiful. Powerful. Engrossing. Uplifting. It's nothing like the shallow, sexual infatuation of movie love.

True love—the real gift of God—is relentless and redemptive. It's selfless, satisfying, and second to nothing. This miracle compels us toward one another, and true love is so good and pure and special that it reaches out and brings into relationship even those who seem unlovable. Love is *that* powerful.

And the miraculous beauty of the God we serve is that love is more than his idea and his invention; it's his identity. God *is* love.[12] So when we love—truly, sacrificially, selflessly—we commune with God himself. And that's a miracle.

Awareness

The more you open up to the mystical reality of Christian life, the more you realize that the miraculous is the common experience, not the exception.

With all the above examples in mind, the question is not *Is the Christian life mystical and miraculous*, but rather *Are we aware of the miracles* and *Do we believe them.*

The Christian mystic prays, "Lord, make me aware. Help me to see what's really real." It's the prayer of those who want to realize and experience God's miraculous power in their lives.

When you ask for it, will you be invited to climb a mountain with Jesus and be visited by long-deceased patriarchs?[13] I doubt it.

Will you see that you're surrounded by a vast flaming army of God's angels?[14] Maybe.

Will you cast out demons and heal others in his name?[15] I hope so!

But a carbon copy of the transfiguration, Elisha's servant's experience, or Paul's act of healing is not the goal. The goal is to become aware of his miraculous power, presence, and activity in the place where *you* are.

I have no doubt that when you ask for these things and wait for God's answer, you will find Jesus' words true:

> And so I tell you, keep on asking, and you will receive what you ask for. Keep on seeking, and you will find. Keep on knocking, and the door will be opened to you. For everyone who asks, receives. Everyone who seeks, finds. And to everyone who knocks, the door will be opened.

You fathers—if your children ask for a fish, do you give them a snake instead? Or if they ask for an egg, do you give them a scorpion? Of course not! So if you sinful people know how to give good gifts to your children, how much more will your heavenly Father give the Holy Spirit to those who ask him. (Luke 11:9-13)

What Happens if You Don't Become a Mystic?

Pierre Teilhard de Chardin said, "We are not human beings having spiritual experiences. We are spiritual beings having human experiences."[16] God did not create us only for biological, physical, measurable experiences. We are created for and capable of so much more.

If we dodge, dismiss, or disbelieve spiritual realities, refusing to believe in the mystical and miraculous, we live half-lives. Lives with a limp. Lives with heads stuck in the sand. Lives that can experience only a tiny slice of what God has so gracefully designed us for.

What's more, when we ignore our spiritual nature—when we are driven by rationalism or emotionalism—we become spiritually blind, and that blindness restricts our humanity.

Mystics see what others cannot, and mystics help heal the world in ways others will not. Those who believe miracles can and do happen are those who witness them. Those who do not believe miss out.

What Happens if You Do Become a Mystic?

I think the most important thing I've learned in the last twenty years of pursuing Jesus is this: God is really real.

I was raised in a Christian home, so if at any point in my life since childhood you asked if I believed in God, a hearty "Of course!" would have been my reply. But believing he's real and experiencing his realness are two very different things.

When, through prayer and faith, you open yourself to the spiritual world God speaks of in the Bible, and when you are filled more and more with the Spirit of God[17], the lights come on. And you begin to see everything the way it really is.

It's like putting on a pair of glasses you didn't realize you needed. But now that everything is clear—the lines are crisp and the colors pop—there's no way you're taking those lenses off.

Becoming a Christian mystic—one who trusts there is far more to life than what can be measured and that true human experience is found in God, not in ourselves—moves you from the sterile, pious, inactive life of disconnected religion, into a heightened, authentic, engaged life of relationship with the God of the universe.

How I Practice Rule #4

A former spiritual director of mine, Alan Fadling[18], taught me a simple process that grows my awareness of God's mystical presence today by remembering miraculous moments with him in my past. Here's how it works and how I practice it.

First, I fought for an hour of silent space with God to reflect on the moments in my life when he showed up or communicated. I asked God to remind me of the most important ones, then I wrote a detailed description of what happened and what I felt during each moment.

Second, I asked God for help identifying a single word or short phrase that summarized each encounter. I asked God these two questions: "What did you say?" and "Why is it important for me?" This took another thirty minutes of silent reflection.

Last, as per Alan's direction, I wrote down those handful of phrases in a prominent place where I can reference them as I spend time listening to Jesus. The phrases he's given over the years are...

- Follow me.
- I love you.
- I'm here.
- Write.
- I'm real.
- Pursue only the King.
- Recover your life.
- Lead at Fellowship North.

There is not space here to unpack the encounter that led to each phrase or the personal meaning of each, but these short sentences spark specific memories of my miracle moments with Jesus. Each time I read them I'm reminded that God has shown up in miraculous ways, and he wants me to remember specific things about him, about me, and about his calling for my life. I'm also reminded that The Holy Spirit showed up and spoke before, so he is present and ready to speak again now.

Here's where the practice of looking back gives me vision for today. Because I can so clearly see the times and places when God showed up in my past, I'm excited to open my heart, mind, eyes, and ears to experience him *today*.

Those experiences encourage me to keep watching and waiting for God to act. They remind me that he is miraculous, and this Christian life is mystical. They help me remember God is really real, he loves me, and he's guiding me into my real life. And that's a reminder I need every single day.

I wonder, when have you been keenly aware of God? When have you been convinced there's something and some*one* bigger, deeper, and better than just what you attain via your five senses? When have you been certain that you are not a human being having spiritual experiences, but a spiritual being having human experiences?

I encourage you to follow along with my practice above. Ask

God to take you back to one of those moments, then remember and record every detail.

These questions may help:

- Where and when did you experience God?
- What details do you remember about the experience?
- Through what or whom did God reveal his presence?
- What did the experience make you feel?
- What do you believe God wants you to remember about that mystical moment?

Now that you've taken the time to recall and revisit the encounter, ask the Father to help you recognize the word or phrase he wants you to hold on to from it.

Spend time with him. Don't rush this.

Once the phrase is clear (this may not happen in one sitting, by the way), record it in a special way and in a prominent place.

Read that phrase and recall the moments in which God gave it to you. Carry it in your mind and heart as you enter space with Jesus this week. Allow that mystical moment from the past to lead you into mystical moments now.

Flashes of heavenly light or mountaintop visions won't necessarily accompany this practice. But that's not the point. What it *will* do is help you connect with God through the memory of your most real moments together.

———

Becoming a mystic, believe it or not, is not about experiencing miracles. It's about realizing that all of life with God is miraculous and living into that reality day after spiritual day.

Rationalism will deprive you of all it means to be human.

Emotionalism will leave you isolated and alone.

Only becoming a Christian mystic who Fights for Space,

Listens to Jesus, and Reads the Bible Slowly, will lead to the full, human life and the dynamic, personal relationship with God you were designed for.

It's these four Rules that make life with God all it's meant to be. Similarly, there are Rules God has given—practices Jesus lived—for life with people. Part Two will unpack the practices and priorities of Jesus that reshape and enliven a Christian life with others.

PART II

RULES FOR LIFE WITH OTHERS

The most important commandment is this: "...You must love the Lord your God with all your heart, all your soul, all your mind, and all your strength."

The second is equally important: "*Love your neighbor* as yourself." No other commandment is greater than these."

— Jesus (Mark 12:29-31)

5

JOIN THE CHURCH

"We must not stand in sheer individualism; once we are Christians, there should be community."
—Francis A. Schaeffer

Did you know you were made to change the world?

That's a loaded question these days. In our narcissistic age, it conjures thoughts of self-empowerment, celebrity, and online influence. Even so, it's true. You *were* made to shape the world.

All of us are made by God to impact our homes, friendships, neighborhoods, churches, cities, and yes, even the world. We just weren't made to do it alone. World-changing is never a solo effort (even if one person tries to take all the credit).

Yet in or increasingly individualized world, few of us realize our full potential. Our cultural infatuation with individualism and our growing dependence on personal technology erodes our ability to sustain intimate relationships within tangible community. As we distance ourselves further and further from others, we have less and less impact.

Several quotes from a "Psychology Today" article capture the reality of our isolation and some of its ramifications.

- Over one-quarter of [American] households consist of people living alone, and this rate is rising.
- From a mental health perspective, the rising individualism...is disturbing. The amassed mental health research indicates that social support, social ties, and community integration act to buffer mental illness and improve mental health. Contrariwise, intense individualism can lead to more isolation, more loneliness, and more alienation.
- Rising individualism has also been implicated in suicide. For example, one study found that districts with rising rates of young male suicide also had the largest rise in the proportion of people living alone, as well as decreasing proportions of married people.[1]

Living the healthy, strong, and influential lives God made us to live becomes increasingly difficult when fewer and fewer people know less and less about us. More of our interpersonal dealings are functional and transactional instead of mutual and committed.

We are solo hikers lost in the woods instead of fellow travelers experiencing the joy of going somewhere together. And we—and our world—are paying the price.

Part(s) of the Problem

The social, relational, and familial distance between us widens for four reasons: our screen addiction, cheap substitutes for real community, self-sufficiency, and sin. Let's look at each.

Addicted to the Screen

On a recent visit to our riverside park, my two children and I were enjoying a beautiful summer morning. The breeze blew, the river sparkled, and we had a blast hunting for different statues in the outdoor sculpture garden together.

While we sat in the grass eating lunch, I felt the emotional pull of my phone. I instinctively reached for it, forgetting for a moment that I locked it safely away in my car (a new habit I'm trying to develop). As I thought about my phone, I took note of how many people around us were focused on screens rather than delighting in the beautiful scenery.

Fifty-one people walked the paths through the park. Forty-three of them stared at a phone.

What's even more interesting—and saddening—is that roughly seventy-five percent of those phone users were *with* other people. Even though they were in the presence of friends, it was their device that held their attention. I thought to myself, *Even when we're together we're alone.*

Look around the next time you're in a restaurant, a waiting room, a house of worship, or even at your own dining room table. What do you see? Almost everyone is glued to the palm-sized screen in their hands or the TV on the wall.

This observation if far from novel. We're all guilty. I had to put strict boundaries on my phone to keep me from texting and driving, ignoring my children, and reaching for it first thing every morning or the last thing every night. So I get it.

This screen addiction decreases our ability to focus on, invest in, and maintain relationships with real people in real time. This is in part why we settle for cheap alternatives to authentic relationships.

Cheap Substitutes

Social media platforms have revolutionized the way the world connects and communicates. Much can be said about the good ways these tools are used to spread awareness, sell products (like this book!), and share virtual events. I'm thankful for the occasional post that makes me laugh, reminds me to pray, or displays an inspired moment of creativity, courage, or compassion.

But with all those positives come plenty of negatives. As with anything else, we must be aware of and faithfully address the dark side of social media use.

Participation on social media often has much to do with the before mentioned addiction. The algorithms and the programmers behind our favorite social media platforms are interested in one thing: capturing your attention for as long as possible so their paying advertisers can sell you something. They are driven by their greed, not your good.[2] And they have us hooked.

I know, I know—I sound like a disconnected curmudgeon. But before you hunker down to defend your usage, let me ask a few questions.

- Do social media platforms *give* you more time with family, neighbors, and close friends—or take it away?
- Does scrolling increase your joy and satisfaction with life, or does the constant competition, comparison, and critique leave you agitated and dissatisfied?
- After a social media binge, do you feel closer to God and connected to community, or are you more distant and alone?

If your answers trend toward the positive side of these question, then great. You've met the challenge of using social media for good and practical purposes rather than a cheap substitute for real community.

But if your honest answers land mostly on the negative side, it's worth evaluating why you use social media and what the true outcomes are.

Screen addiction and social media, however, are the fruit of deeper cultural problems, starting with individualism and self-sufficiency.

Self-Sufficiency

Western culture's primary indoctrination is about self-sufficiency. We're tempted by the shows we watch, articles we read, technology we use, and even some of the sermons we hear to believe that life is a solo enterprise, and we can make it on our own.

But this frame of mind bears dark fruit. The statistics on suicide, anxiety, and depression are dismal.[3] Anyone without meaningful relationships is in danger of suffering the consequences of isolation and loneliness. It turns out, the god of individualism and self-reliance is not a good god to serve. It eats its faithful alive.

Underneath each of these, is humanity's original dilemma. Our slide toward isolation is facilitated by sin.

Sin

Sin is a word that has all but disappeared from Americans' vocabulary. Even our churches use the word less and less.

The loss of the vocabulary word is symptomatic of a much more disturbing reality: Many deny the spiritual truth that there are immoral acts that transgress God's divine law. The idea that human beings rebel against a holy God is passé.

But we must face the music. The underlying reason for our disconnected, selfish egocentricity is a refusal to align our hearts, minds, and actions with God's good way. And that is sin.

God created us for constant communion with him and other people, but in our sinfulness we reject both. And it continues to leave us marooned.

———

When we get sucked into an addicted, self-reliant life and become dependent on cheap substitutes for true community, we lose more than just real relationships. We also lose our meaning and purpose. Sin disconnects us from our distinct design as a community of God's image bearers.

We were created for more than an inner-focused, egocentric, me-myself-and-I kind of life. *Way* more.

We were created to catch the vision of the Master, respond to his invitation to "follow me,"[4] and walk into the world arm-in-arm with God and his other followers to fight epic battles, live deep moments, and partner in making the world a thriving and beautiful place.

Fishing Together

There's this spectacular moment at the outset of Jesus' ministry in which a small group of men caught the same vision at the same time.

The Gospel of Luke tells us that Jesus drew a large crowd as he taught along the shores of the Sea of Galilee. He spotted Simon Peter's fishing vessel and asked him to push them out into the water so his voice would carry to the throng on the beach.

After teaching for a bit, Jesus decided it was time for a more private and powerful moment. We pick up the story there:

> When he had finished speaking, he said to Simon, "Now go out where it is deeper, and let down your nets to catch some fish."
>
> "'Master," Simon replied, "we worked hard all last night and

didn't catch a thing. But if you say so, I'll let the nets down again."
(Luke 5:4-5)

I can imagine Peter (also called Simon or Simon Peter) thinking, "What does this teacher know about fishing?" Andrew, his
brother, was already convinced Jesus was the Messiah,[5] but Peter
wasn't yet sure. To Peter's credit, he swallowed his professional
pride and heeded the Rabbi's request, and this is what happened...

This time their nets were so full of fish they began to tear! A shout
for help brought their partners in the other boat, and soon both
boats were filled with fish and on the verge of sinking.

When Simon Peter realized what had happened, he fell to his
knees before Jesus and said, "Oh, Lord, please leave me—I'm
such a sinful man." For he was awestruck by the number of fish
they had caught, as were the others with him. His partners,
James and John, the sons of Zebedee, were also amazed. (Luke
5:6-10)

Can you picture Peter and Andrew—then James and John—
dumbfounded by the haul of fish? It's difficult to imagine this kind
of miracle today, but it's fun to try.

If you're a car salesman, imagine the Spirit of God showing up
at your car lot and bringing two hundred and fifty people ready to
buy cars—for cash—without even test-driving!

If you're a waiter, imagine Jesus taking a table during your shift,
then watching as every patron leaves you a $1000 tip, for a full
eight-hour shift, ten shifts in a row.

Or imagine being an architect and opening up your computer
on Monday morning to find all your current projects—plus fifty
new ones—fully designed and ready for construction, with clients
having already paid in full. Then up pops an email from Jesus that
says, "Good morning!" with a thumbs up emoji.

There's no doubt your response would be much like Peter's. He realized and confessed his unworthiness on the spot. He knew he didn't belong in the same boat as the Son of God.

Jesus' response to Peter is life-changing: "Don't be afraid! From now on you'll be fishing for people!"[6] And with that, Jesus persuaded Peter and the boys to join his mission to invite people into the kingdom of God.

But notice how their new fishing job will be done: *together*. Jesus' words were an explicit invitation into a *community*. A team. A crew. A brotherhood and sisterhood on a mission together to love God, love each other, and invite anyone and everyone else to get to know Jesus with them.

And the Bible tells us they accepted the invitation. "And as soon as they landed, they left everything and followed Jesus."[7]

Fishing with Love

Fast forward to the end of Jesus' Earth-bound ministry. Those first followers—the men through whom Jesus created his Church[8] —were still at his side. Just hours before Jesus saved the world through his death, the Son of God gave them a new commandment:

> So now I am giving you a new commandment: Love each other. Just as I have loved you, you should love each other. Your love for one another will prove to the world that you are my disciples. (John 13:34-35)

They were all-in on Jesus and each other, but the completion of their training centered on a "new commandment." The commandment wasn't to work miracles, heal the sick, fight evil, or travel far and wide. They did those things, but it was the fresh command to love one another as Jesus loved them that glued them to God and each other. They were to give themselves—holding absolutely nothing back—to Jesus and one another.

But here's the thing: Their love for each other did not end with them. The ultimate end of their Jesus-centered, communal love was the inclusion of others into their tribe of servant-leadership and sacrificial love. Jesus said, "Your love for one another will prove to the world that you are my disciples."[9] They were to become fishers of people.

And more than their miracles, preaching, writing, or martyrdom, it was their love for one another that would compel others toward Christ.

That is the community God built. It's one centered on sacrificial love and unbound inclusion. It's a remarkably *un*-selfish tribe of followers who exemplify the way of Jesus among each other. It's the Church. And God's desire is for all of us to join.

Big "C" Church

Before we explore the word "join," let's define the Church. Here are the four definitions according to the Oxford Languages dictionary via Google:

noun: church; plural noun: churches

1. *a building used for public Christian worship. I.e. "they came to church with me"*
2. *a particular Christian organization, typically one with its own clergy, buildings, and distinctive doctrines. I.e. "I belong to the Methodist church."*
3. *the hierarchy of clergy of a Christian organization, especially the Roman Catholic Church or the Church of England. I.e. "leaders of the church met for another council last February"*
4. *institutionalized religion as a political or social force. I.e. "the separation of church and state"*

Notice that each definition revolves around the words "building", "organization", or "institution". These are the meanings of the word church for most English speakers today. But there's the English definition of words, and there's the *biblical* definition of words.

To understand the Church and why joining in is Rule #5 for a Christian life, we must grasp the definition for "church" in its original biblical language, ancient Greek.

Church People

Ekklesia is the ancient Greek word that's translated "church" in your English Bible.[10] It's found over a hundred times in the New Testament, and it always refers to one thing: an assembly of *people*.

Ekklesia is not specifically a religious word. It refers to any group of people gathered for a purpose. What makes an *ekklesia* the Church of Jesus Christ is that the people who gather believe and declare Jesus is Savior and Lord, and they are filled with God himself, the Holy Spirit. And their purpose, is his purpose.

Contrary to today's dictionary definition of church, the Bible never refers to the word "church" as a place, building, institution, or organization. It is *always* a people.

Pastor and author Jeff Vanderstelt describes *ekklesia* as "the regenerate people of God saved by the power of God for the purposes of God in this world."[11] His definition is worth looking at closely.

The Regenerate People of God

Regenerate means reborn, reformed, or renewed. Literally regenerated. The Apostle Paul wrote, "anyone who belongs to Christ has become a new person. The old life is gone; a new life has begun!"[12]

Those who surrender their lives to God, through faith in Jesus

Christ, to be filled by the Holy Spirit, are reborn.[13] Their trusting belief in Jesus justifies them before God and begins a process of Spirit-powered transformation.

The Church is the regenerate people of God.

Saved by the Power of God

Because of sin, those who do not trust Jesus' restorative work are doomed to complete separation from God. It's a present-day hell and an everlasting one.

But those who receive God's love, confess their sinfulness, believe the life-saving work of Jesus, and submit to him as Lord, are saved from separation from God into the family of God.

This salvation is accomplished by God through Jesus on our behalf. We can't earn it, accomplish it, or deserve it by our own merit or energies. [14]

The Church is people saved by the power of God.

For the Purposes of God in this World

The New Testament word *ekklesia* denotes an assembled group of Jesus followers who are sent out into the world for a very special purpose: to accomplish God's plans.

God gives his Spirit to his Church to partner with him for his kingdom to come and his will to be done on Earth.[15] We are representatives of him and for him[16] for the sake of all others.

The Church is a regenerate people, saved by God alone, to continue the work of Jesus and accomplish his purposes in this world.

———

Author Ruth Haley Barton describes the Church like this: "Christian community is made of people who gather around the transforming presence of Christ so they can do the will of God."[17]

That is the Church I am encouraging you to join. It's the spiritually and physically assembled people of God around the world and in your neighborhood with whom Christians join to participate in God's action in the world. In so doing they experience the full life—the *real* life—God has blueprinted for them.

But the question remains, what does it mean to *join* this Church? And why will it matter?

What Do You Mean "Join"?

The large majority of Christian churches in America invite their participants to become members or "join" their congregation. And, for the record, there's nothing wrong with official "church membership."

But membership is not what I mean by Rule #5, Join the Church. I mean actively engaging with others in the mission of God. And how do you actively engage in God's mission with other Christians? You participate, commit, identify, and extend.

Participate

The very first followers of Jesus—those who became the first-century Church—did not have a membership course. They had tangible ways to participate.

"Participate in what?" you might ask. They participated in the things they knew God loves and does, wherever, whenever, and with whomever he was doing it.

The second chapter of Acts describes how they participated together:

All the believers devoted themselves to the apostles' teaching, and to fellowship, and to sharing in meals (including the Lord's Supper) and to prayer. A deep sense of awe came over them all, and the apostles performed many miraculous signs and wonders. And all the believers met together in one place and shared everything they had. They sold their property and possessions and shared the money with those in need. They worshiped together at the Temple each day, met in homes for the Lord's Supper, and shared their meals with great joy and generosity—all the while praising God and enjoying the goodwill of all the people. And each day the Lord added to their fellowship those who were being saved. (Acts 2:42-47)

The first followers of Jesus were outsiders. There was no such thing as a Christian country or a moral majority or "evangelicalism." They were simply men and women who responded with passionate gratitude to Jesus' work in their lives, even in the face of fierce persecution.

They participated to be faithful, not popular. They participated to obey Jesus' Great Commission,[18] to grow spiritually, and to engage with God's Spirit-enlivened community.

There's a Jesus-focused, gospel-centered, Bible-preaching group of believers somewhere near you that cares about loving your community in wonderful ways. Find them. Participate with them. And witness how things—and people—change.

Once you join God's people through participation, the next step is to join them through commitment.

Commit

I began with participation rather than commitment because commitment without participation is only lip service. Get your hands dirty first, then take the next step and commit.

When my family began participating with our church, it was a stressed and struggling body of believers. My wife and I had no idea at first. We arrived from out of town unaware of the roles and relationships, history and hardship that made up this group of Jesus followers. All we knew was that God kept confirming—specifically through people, promptings, and peace—that this was our new church home.

Despite the difficulties they faced, this congregation of believers followed hard after God. So, in our commitment to obey God, we committed ourselves to these people. Our journey from first-time visitors to spiritual leaders began with participation and commitment.

Participation with and commitment to a local church is not about what it offers you. It's about how you can join with them by using your gifts and resources to accomplish God's purposes together.

If you listen to Jesus while you search for and participate with other Christians, he will guide you.

First you participate, second you commit. And the third step to Join the Church seals your connection to the people with whom you now belong. That step is identification.

Identify

True identification with others in God's family happens by honestly and vulnerably sharing your story. Admitting you are human, and knowing and accepting others as imperfect humans, connects you.

As I alluded to above, my wife and I knew no one when we moved to Arkansas. And I mean *nobody*. Once we found this small, local church, we slowly made a few friends. After some time, we started to get together regularly with a few other families to live out our faith within community.

The best decision our new group ever made was to follow Jesus together, come what may, no matter what. The *second* best decision we made was to put all our ignorance and brokenness, losses and victories on full display by sharing our personal stories of faith with each other.

The first couple to share set the bar for the rest of us. And they pulled no punches. They flung the doors of their lives and windows into their souls wide open. They told us about their lost battles, their insecurities, their failures, and their sinful bent toward selfishness.

They also shared how God met them in each and every one of those dark corners. They laughed and they cried.

The rest of us listened with rapt attention. We were moved by their bravery, and relieved that by their example we were given permission to talk openly about or own warts, bruises, and gaping wounds. We were awed by how good God was to them and reminded how good God was to us.

A couple months later, after sharing all our stories, we were bonded. We identified with one another. Vulnerability was the glue that held us together from the beginning.

We must be a people who share our stories, in all their glory and gruesomeness, to experience what it means to be family. Identification with others through vulnerability and truth-telling helps us become known, develop empathy, and realize we are not alone. Each is a building block for true, mutual relationship and becoming part of a people who impact our world.

You involuntarily join God's Church the moment you allow Jesus to be your King. You *voluntarily* join the Church when you participate, commit, and identify with other Jesus followers around you.

The final step of voluntary membership is to extend yourself.

Extend

I believe extending ourselves is the step of joining the Church most closely aligned to God's heart. As I type these words, I can't help but think of the hymn Paul penned in Philippians 2:3-7.

> Don't be selfish; don't try to impress others. Be humble, thinking of others as better than yourselves. Don't look out only for your own interests, but take an interest in others, too.
>
> You must have the same attitude that Christ Jesus had. Though he was God, he did not think of equality with God as something to cling to. Instead, he gave up his divine privileges; he took the humble position of a slave and was born as a human being.

Jesus gave up everything. He took an unimaginable demotion to participate with us, commit to us, identify with us, and extend grace to us. It's the truest picture of what being the Church is all about.

When we extend ourselves for the sake of one another, human disconnection is destroyed, and we become who we were meant to be.

This happens individually as you sacrifice your own way for his, and it happens corporately as all of God's people extend themselves in love toward each other then out into the world.

There is a myriad of ways to extend yourself for another's sake. I'll cover more of them in Rule #6 and Rule #7, but all of them begin with an extension of God's grace to one another.

Grace, compassion, empathy, and forgiveness hold us together. Why? Because the Church is a hospital of the sick, not a museum of the perfect.[19] The variety among us and the sin that plagues us are, in some ways, no different from any other group of humans.

The difference is, the Church *knows* we are sick. We turn to God alone for our healing. We understand that extending grace to one another on our journey toward greater wholeness is the way of Jesus.

God himself is in us, and he is on full display and operating at full power when we are agents of his grace toward one another. Jesus said it so very well, "Your love for one another will prove to the world that you are my disciples."[20]

What Happens if You Don't Join the Church?

Do you know anyone who says, "I can follow Jesus alone; I don't need the church"? Maybe you've said it. Maybe you believe it.

Because I love you, let me be straightforward: It's a lie. The idea of following Jesus alone is a dangerous deception that the enemy of God wants you to believe so you won't participate in the world-changing good that comes through God's Church.

I've often said that our faith in Jesus is personal, but it is not private. When we try to individualize our relationship with Jesus we dishonor and disobey his command to serve others and make disciples together.

Beyond the failure to participate corporately, we also experience problems individually.

Without joining the Church, we are susceptible to cultural intoxication. The currents of rationalism and emotionalism are strong, and without the church you will adopt the culture's values without even knowing it. It's by participating and pursuing truth together that we protect each other from our own wandering religious ideas and hopes.

Finally, the growth and progression of your spiritual life depends on your engagement with other believers. Without engaging with others, you will stagnate. Real, deep growth is facilitated by trying and failing with the love and encouragement of others on the journey with Jesus.

Attempting to live your faith life on your own results in isolation, lack of true growth, weakened and heretical faith, and stunted experience with God. Is that the faith *you* want?

What Happens if You Do Join the Church?

Jesus taught his disciples to pray "Your kingdom come, your will be done, on earth as it is in heaven."[21] His prayer is for a present-tense reality, not a future-tense destination, and God's Church experiences his kingdom *today*. And together, we bring his kingdom to the world.

God's instructions set a foundation of behavior that leads his family to rich, full, powerful, and peaceful living. And when acted upon together, they show a watching world just how good it is to live in God's kingdom and presence here and now.

On an individual note, God promises that you will never be alone as a follower of Jesus. Join his Church and you will experience his presence—through other people—in the most tangible of ways. Nothing pushes back the negative impact of isolated and individualized living like joining the people of God in the work of God.

And together we can change the world.

How I Practice Rule #5

I won't lie to you. It's difficult to participate, commit, identify, and extend yourself with the people of God. I'm a Christian writer and a church pastor and still find it challenging. But this says more about the influence of our culture and the selfishness of my heart than it does about the goodness of God's design.

The harder and longer I try, and the more sacrificial and unselfish my approach is, the more beautiful and fruitful life together becomes. To date, participating, committing, identifying, and extending myself with a gospel-centered group of fellow believers, is one of the most vital practices of my life with God.

At our best, our church family—and our group of Christian friends—walks the way of Jesus together. Formally and informally, regularly and seasonally, we join forces to love God, love others, and make disciples of Jesus.[22] Like the earliest of disciples, we attempt to devote ourselves to Jesus and the apostles' teaching, to fellowship, to sharing meals (including the Lord's Supper), and to prayer.[23]

At our worst, we resort to avoiding the mission of God and each other, opting for the "privacy" of our narcissistic and fast-paced society. Down that road we find more loneliness and less laughter, more minutia and less mission, and we miss out on the chance to partner with God in remaking his world.

Like all the practices recommended in this book, joining the Church requires patient intentionality. Giving up our way to adopt God's way[24] is a slow, moment-by-moment, day-by-day process, but it's *worth the effort.*

If you are not yet participating with a local church and some gospel-centered friendships, I encourage you to keep praying and trying.

Ask God plainly and often to help you find a gospel-centered church and to build friendships there. Then try—and I mean try hard—to do both.

I don't mean be annoying or anxious. I mean be deliberate and patient. As God reveals to you the people with whom you might grow in spiritual friendship, take steps to engage with them and Jesus. Engage in—and even prepare your mind and heart to lead— kingdom focused activities with others.

If you're new to this, it can be as simple as asking a fellow Christian to pray together sometime, or to read a book of the Bible together and discuss its daily impact on your life. Commit to attend a church service together and share lunch after, or pursue a community group experience like I wrote of above.

Whatever it is, it will only happen if you make a prayerful and intentional effort. But worry not: God will answer your prayer and reward your effort.

———

Joining the Church is rarely easy. Yet, the joys of sharing life and participating in the mission of God outweigh the difficulties. The glory it brings to God, the service it is to others, and the way in which God uses us to change the world is worth every bit of blood, sweat, and tears.

As I participate, commit, identify, and extend myself in our local church, God continues to develop me in ways I could never develop on my own. I encourage you to look for (or create) a Christ-centered group of people with whom you can participate in God's kingdom, and don't give up until you have them. You need the Church, and we need you.

And when you find them, allow the Spirit of God to set you on mission for his glory and others' good. Make a pact together to commit to this Rule and the Rules that follow. You won't be sorry.

6

DON'T JUST SING THERE

"Don't let your life give evidence against your tongue. Sing with your voices... sing also with your conduct."
—St. Augustine of Hippo

Has anyone ever invited you to "join them for worship?" Or asked, "Where do you worship on Sundays?"

When our family relocated from California to Arkansas, quite a few folks in our new and hospitable Bible-belt town asked us those exact questions. And I'm quite happy about that. As you know from the previous chapter, gathering as the Church is important stuff.

But the more I understand what the Bible says about worship, the less I understand those two questions. I know what they mean culturally—but I'm less and less sure what they mean biblically or theologically.

Culturally, the phrase "Come worship with us!" is an invitation to visit a Sunday service. The word "worship" in this context—and many others—means a public event for Christians at a church building. The event or service includes music, preaching, corporate prayer, or a variety of other liturgical elements. The full ceremony and all its accouterments are a "worship" service.

At least, that's *one* definition.

But in many Western protestant traditions, the definition of worship is even narrower. Worship is synonymous with music.

Whether that music is sung during the obligatory thirty-minute set before the sermon or as a God-centered life soundtrack pumped through earbuds, music about God is referred to as "worship" music.

It is primarily those songs—and the accompanying act of joining in—that we think of today when we hear the word "worship."

A Christian artist can release a "worship" album, and we all know it's church music. It's how the woman who leads the music at your Sunday gatherings got the title "Worship Leader." The worship leader is not the head pastor, the elders, or even the "host" of the service. The worship leader is the one who leads the singing.

Though many Christians and church leaders would not explicitly claim that music or singing is the sole definition of worship, our practice, which is belief lived out in behavior, implies otherwise. For many of us, worship is restricted to the music portion of our faith lives.

Unfortunately, this limited definition of worship is not what the Bible has in mind. It's incomplete at best, heretical at worst. So, we've got to take a much closer look at what we mean when we invite others to worship with us.

Meaningful Music

Yes, you might wonder, but haven't God's people been singing praises as a form of worship since the beginning? Aren't we called to make a joyful noise to the Lord and sing his praises every day?[1]

Yes, and amen. In fact, it's difficult to overestimate the value of music in the human experience as a whole. God made humans with music in our bones. The people of God are no exception. We are designed to enjoy it, appreciate it, and be moved by it. We hum it, sing it, whistle it, and dance to it.

And lest you think I hate church music or haven't read much of my Bible, I fully acknowledge that an integral expression of joy in the Lord, gratitude for his gifts, and praise for his character is expressed through song.

In fact, all through the pages of the Bible God's people respond to him through music and singing and encouraging others to do the same. Here are a few examples.

In the Old Testament, singers performed together to praise and give thanks to the Lord. Accompanied by trumpets, cymbals, and other instruments, they raised their voices and praised the LORD with these words: "He is good! His faithful love endures forever!"[2]

The Psalms, of course, are a collection of songs and poetry that have been sung to the Lord for thousands of years. It's been called the Bible's Song Book.

Then, in the New Testament, an important part of Christian gatherings in the first century was singing and music. Jesus' followers sang "psalms and hymns and spiritual songs to God with thankful hearts."[3] Paul's letters include portions of these hymns, printed for you to see—and sing—today.[4]

And the list goes on.

Music from both biblical and extra-biblical accounts[5] was part of the fabric of Christian life together and Christian worship of God. They did it then, we do it now.

In fact, large portions of the music consumed in various time periods—be it Christian or not—was created by people who believed in God, some of whom were followers of Jesus. Music has always been a powerful, beautiful, and dynamic part of Christian living.

But as big a part of the Christian life as music is, true worship is much bigger.

Worship: God's Definition

It's obvious from the biblical record that music and singing are not, by themselves, the problem. So what is?

The problem is not the practice of singing as worship, but the priority given to it as the *definition* of worship. We make a dangerous misstep if we define worship as only music and singing.

Paul's letter to the Romans includes God's definition of worship.

> I urge you, brothers and sisters, in view of God's mercy, to offer your bodies as a living sacrifice, holy and pleasing to God—this is your true and proper worship. (Romans 12:1)

We can draw a handful of important conclusions about worship from this one verse. First, biblical worship is a response to God. Paul exhorts his brothers and sisters to worship "in view of God's mercy."

In Romans 11 Paul explains how God, in essence, works out everything so that he can and will have mercy on all who trust him. This is good news for all who know how sorely they need God's grace.

Second, biblical worship is both personal and corporate. Paul wrote Romans to a group of believers, his "brothers and sisters"—*plural*—in Rome. Likewise the word "bodies" is plural. So Paul is urging this group of Jesus followers to give themselves to God, both as individual persons *and* as an interconnected group of people.

Yet the instruction is deeply personal. The group can offer itself corporately only if all the individuals offer themselves individually.

Here's the crux: Biblical worship is a "living sacrifice." I can't help but wonder if this confused Paul's original audience. They knew about dead sacrifices. Animal sacrifice was common in both the Jewish religious practice and Greco-Roman polytheistic religions. But Paul wrote about something altogether different.

First, his declaration is an oxymoron. *Living* sacrifices. Living *sacrifices*. These two don't go together. But Paul was a brilliant writer, and his metaphor works.

Worship as a living sacrifice is *sacrificial living*. It's a moment-by-moment, day-by-day, year-in and year-out volunteering of all our mind's thoughts and our body's actions to him and for him.

Does this kind of living include our singing and Sunday services? Of course. Can it be restricted to our music and gatherings? Not a chance.

A Picture of Empty Religion

Two encounters from Jesus' life put flesh and blood on the biblical idea of worship. One gives an example of what worship is *not*. Let's start there.

Jesus confronted the religious leaders of his day on a regular basis. Not all were bad, but many missed the point. And Jesus pointed that out, for their sake and the sake of those they influenced.

Matthew includes one such confrontation. Jesus starts by warning his followers about the errant way of these religious leaders, then he confronts the leaders themselves. Jesus' words show us what true worship is not:

> Jesus said to the crowds and to his disciples, "The teachers of religious law and the Pharisees are the official interpreters of the law of Moses. So practice and obey whatever they tell you, but don't follow their example. For they don't practice what they teach. They crush people with unbearable religious demands and never lift a finger to ease the burden.
>
> "Everything they do is for show. On their arms they wear extra wide prayer boxes with Scripture verses inside, and they wear robes with extra long tassels. And they love to sit at the head table at banquets and in the seats of honor in the synagogues. They

love to receive respectful greetings as they walk in the market-places, and to be called "Rabbi.""" (Matthew 23:1-7)

The religious leaders Jesus spoke of embodied the word hypocrite. They taught one thing but lived another. It's why Jesus could say, "Practice and obey whatever they tell you, but don't follow their example."[6]

They were like a lung doctor who chain smokes. What they taught others about life with God was good and true, but they failed to live it themselves.

It's why Jesus pulled no punches when he confronted them moments later. His long, scathing rebuke included these words:

> What sorrow awaits you teachers of religious law and you Pharisees. Hypocrites! For you are careful to tithe even the tiniest income from your herb gardens, but you ignore the more important aspects of the law—justice, mercy, and faith. You should tithe, yes, but do not neglect the more important things. Blind guides! You strain your water so you won't accidentally swallow a gnat, but you swallow a camel!
>
> What sorrow awaits you teachers of religious law and you Pharisees. Hypocrites! For you are so careful to clean the outside of the cup and the dish, but inside you are filthy—full of greed and self-indulgence! (Matthew 23:23-25)

Technically, these men did the right religious things. For example, they gave a specific percentage of their income—a tithe—to the poor. But they didn't relinquish their lives in full to God, neglecting what he cared about most: justice, mercy, and faith.

In a modern-day context, these are hoarder-types who preach about generosity, or sexual deviants who teach chastity, or marriage counselors who have affairs. They sing worship songs on Sunday but fail to surrender their lives on Monday.

Jesus used their bad example to reiterate his regular refrain:

"The greatest among you must be a servant. But those who exalt themselves will be humbled, and those who humble themselves will be exalted."[7]

Biblical worship is deeper than religious activity.

A Picture of True Worship

Later in Luke's gospel, we receive a picture of worship, and it stands in bold contrast to the religious legalism of the Pharisees. Jesus commented on a woman who gave her life over to God, trusting him with the results. She was a woman who worshiped. And her simple act was far more than religious practice.

> While Jesus was in the Temple, he watched the rich people dropping their gifts in the collection box. Then a poor widow came by and dropped in two small coins.
>
> "I tell you the truth," Jesus said, "this poor widow has given more than all the rest of them. For they have given a tiny part of their surplus, but she, poor as she is, has given everything she has." (Luke 21:1-4)

It's a mistake to think this vignette is only about money. Yes, the woman gave her money, but simultaneously she surrendered her life.

How do I know? Because the only person you give *all* your remaining money to is someone you deeply trust. This poor widow —who would have been unable to create income on her own— trusted God to provide. Her devotion to him was on full display that day.

The point here is not the money. If it was, Jesus would not have bragged on her for giving "more" than the rich folk when actually she gave less. The point, it seems, is the extent to which someone's giving represents their posture towards God and their trust in him.

The woman was poor in material possession but rich on

personal surrender. She had little wealth but worshipped truly. The others' pockets were deep, but it didn't mean their worship was.

The difference between giving some of yourself and giving all of yourself is the difference between worship as a compartmentalized act (like singing or giving money) and a sacrificial lifestyle (which can include plenty of singing and loads of generosity!). The rich folk who gave a ton of cash exemplified one, and the woman who gave two small coins exemplified another.

The Problem

Here's what's at stake when worship through music becomes the *sole* expression of worship: It's a cop-out, a checklist, culturally limited, and a poor witness. Allow me to explain each.

It's a cop-out.

Surrendering your life to God is much more difficult than singing to him (and for those of you that *hate* to sing, that's saying something).

Given the option to let God redirect all our time, passions, and loves—or just join in the weekly Christian sing-along—most of us will choose the latter and call it good.

When our definition is limited to Sunday singing or crooning in the car, we rob God of the true and complete worship he's due. And we deprive ourselves of the true blessing—the real life—it is to give our lives back to the One who created them.

It's a checklist.

When worship is narrowly defined as music and singing, it becomes a momentary event rather than an ongoing way of being. But worship is not a checklist, it's a *lifestyle*.

If singing is all there is of worship, it becomes a transaction in which the right kinds of songs earn God's approval. But it's not that easy, because life's not cheap. It's not that limited, because God is infinite. It's not that impersonal, because God is love. Relationship with God is a humble life of freedom through surrender, not a moral contract.

Worship is anything you do to please God, *and* worship is the way you do everything because you are so pleased with God. And a life completely turned over to God is the most true, pure, brilliant life there is: one that's far more—and far better— than some religious to-do list.

It's culturally limited.

If worship is defined as music, then who determines what type of music, which talented musician, or what kind of service is the truest worship of God?

Think about this: If God's definition of worship is singing and music alone, then worship is culturally—not universally—defined. After all, "good" singing and "great" music are in the ear of the beholder.

Does the God of the universe have an ear for today's hip hop or thirties big band? Is God a classical guy or a jazz aficionado? Does he love African, South American, Asian, or European music the most?

If worship is truly limited to music, then we should all just sing the Psalms. After all, those are the timeless tunes ensconced in the actual Word of God.

It's a poor witness.

If Jesus followers limit the worship of God to musical expression, we rob the world of true Christian witness. The Church bears witness to the fact that there's a good and loving God—

seen perfectly in Jesus—who is the source of authentic human life.

When we limit our worship to singing, we deny the reality that we are all created to worship and that every human being will—consciously or subconsciously—surrender to some thing, someone, or some idea.

Christians who define worship as a weekly song service reveal that they don't actually worship God at all. They commit time to a religious ritual, but the true devotion of their life is given to something or someone else.

This is a weak witness to the reality and necessity of a relationship with the living God. Singing to our good God is a sign of affection, but if it's our only expression of worship, it leaves us—and a watching world—needing much more.

———

All these dangers simply disappear when worship is defined as the full, sacrificial surrender of life to the God who created you, loves you, and wants you.

Jesus lived the worshipful life by doing nothing except what God told him to do. After healing a man and receiving some pushback for it, Jesus explained it like this:

> I tell you the truth, the Son can do nothing by himself. He does only what he sees the Father doing. Whatever the Father does, the Son also does. For the Father loves the Son and shows him everything he is doing. In fact, the Father will show him how to do even greater works than healing this man. Then you will truly be astonished. (John 5:19-20)

This, my friend, is worship. Jesus never wavered in his commitment to do whatever the Father asked. His life was a living sacrifice, and he did whatever it took to live out the salvation plan for your sake and mine. Even when that meant his death.

In our egocentric individualized culture, this may not seem like living. But surrendering to the God of the Bible does not compromise the good life; it *creates* the good life.

Working for the Lord

Paul's additional description of worship in Colossians is another timely and crucial word from God.

> Work willingly at whatever you do, as though you were working for the Lord rather than for people. Remember that the Lord will give you an inheritance as your reward, and that the Master you are serving is Christ. (Colossians 3:23-24)

Paul's instruction here aligns so perfectly with his definition of worship in Romans 12:1 that he repeats it twice in the third chapter of Colossians. In verse seventeen he wrote, "*Whatever* you do or say, do it as a representative of the Lord Jesus."[8]

In other words, in every corner of your life—spiritual, family, and work life—live in submission to and on behalf of Jesus. God calls you to put aside your cultural and personal notions about life and fully embrace that everything you do, big or small, is an offering to him. Your life is made for worship.

This is a lovely idea, right? What Christian wouldn't like to proudly claim that everything he does, from the smallest favor to the biggest job, the briefest look to the longest conversation, is done for God?

But what does it really look like to work for the Lord rather than people? After all, your uptight manager, checked-out spouse, annoying friend, and dysfunctional church family aren't making it any easier.

Worshipping God by working for the Lord is both action and

outcome. It's the willful act of submission *and* the natural outcome of prayerful preparation. It all comes back to the first chapters of this book.

- *Do you fight for space?* – Do you prioritize silence and stillness in your daily grind? Do you turn off your phone, make quiet space, and settle your mind to connect with God?
- *Do you listen for Jesus?* – Do you pay attention to the Creator and practice recognizing his voice? Do you adopt practices that tune you in to God's constant presence and dialogue?
- *Do you read the Bible slowly?* – Is God's Word central to your times of space and attempts to listen? Do you read for formation or information? Are you open to the possibility and promise that God can transform you by his Word?
- *Are you a mystic?* – Do you believe God is far more than what can be measured, and far truer and better than just what you feel? Are you beginning to let go of the "isms" and ideas that prevent you from going all-in on God?
- *Have you joined the Church?* – Do you pray for and seek out ways to connect with and contribute to the work of God's people where you are? Do you join in the work they are doing to live lives sacrificed for him together?

It's a lot of questions, but they're the most important ones.

When you engage God in these spiritual disciplines, he opens avenues in your life to realize he is present, to understand what he says, and be filled with his Spirit. In doing so, you become capable of working for the Lord, whether you're contributing to a thriving group of Christians, serving your family and friends, or becoming the very best employee or employer possible.

You Can't Fake It

Anyone who knows you well can name what you worship. It's whichever person, possession, or pursuit you prioritize with your money, time, and thoughts. Anyone can offer lip service to God on the weekend, but it's the moments between that reveal our true devotion.

Jesus made that point when he chastised the religious elite. He said,

> You hypocrites! Isaiah was right when he prophesied about you, for he wrote, "These people honor me with their lips, but their hearts are far from me. Their worship is a farce, for they teach man-made ideas as commands from God." (Matthew 15:7-9)

When our worship is only with our lips, it's a farce. But the gratitude-filled giving of your whole self to him is the opposite of a farce. It's the living and holy sacrifice that God receives as an acceptable and pleasing act of worship.

The author of Hebrews summed it up quite well.

> Let us offer through Jesus a continual sacrifice of praise to God, proclaiming our allegiance to his name. And don't forget to do good and to share with those in need. These are the sacrifices that please God.[9]

Worship is action that proves our allegiance. Worship is a life lived fully invested in God's greatest commandments: "Love the Lord your God with all your heart, all your soul, and all your mind" and "Love your neighbor as yourself." (Hebrews 13:15-16)

This kind of worship—the kind that is complete, sacrificial allegiance—is the kind you can't fake. And in God's great economy, it's the kind of life that is the real, full life Jesus promised.

If any of you wants to be my follower, you must give up your own way, take up your cross, and follow me. If you try to hang on to your life, you will lose it. But if you give up your life for my sake and for the sake of the good news, you will save it. And what do you benefit if you gain the whole world but lose your own soul? Is anything worth more than your soul? (Mark 8:35-37)

What Happens if Your Worship is Only Singing?

If we limit our "worship" to any one religious activity—be it singing, or church attendance, or studying the Bible, or praying, or volunteering—we will miss out on the remarkable life God has for us. Because believe it or not, a life returned to God is not a life in which things are taken away from you—it's a life in which everything is given to you.

When you limit your definition of worship, you limit your ability to experience the God who is worthy of your true worship. If a song is all you give, you will only receive an echo in return. But if you give all of your life, you will receive all of his life. And the goodness of that is virtually incomprehensible.

What Happens if Your Worship is a Living Sacrifice?

We found the written definition of worship in the first verse of Romans 12. It's important for us to read it again, this time along with verse two. Check this out:

And so, dear brothers and sisters, I plead with you to give your bodies to God because of all he has done for you. Let them be a living and holy sacrifice—the kind he will find acceptable. This is truly the way to worship him. Don't copy the behavior and customs of this world, but let God transform you into a new person by changing the way you think. Then you will learn to know God's will for you, which is good and pleasing and perfect. (Romans 12:1-2)

Worship—that is, living sacrificially—is the gateway to a transformed life. It's the activity through which we discover God's good, pleasing, and perfect will for us.

And at the end of the day, these are the two things human beings are most thirsty for: a transformed life, one that's beyond what they can fabricate on their own, and a life that's on the right track, fulfilling the true design and purpose for which it was made.

When you and I surrender our lives to God, this is what we get.

How I Practice Rule #6

Living a life of sacrifice to God—true worship—is so comprehensive that it's difficult to describe just one practice to help you live it out. But here are two places to start: Practice using the word "worship" correctly, and/or do something different on Sunday mornings. Both have helped me refocus my energies on giving all of my life to God in various seasons.

Change the Way You Speak

Language matters. What we hear and say shapes the way we think, which shapes the way we behave. We will talk about this phenomenon more in Rule #8, Redefine Love, but the idea will bear fruit here as you change the way you think about worship.

For the past several years now, I've assigned more accurate language to congregational singing, Sunday gatherings of God's church, and the act of worship. Old habits die hard, so you can still catch me inviting folks to join me for "Sunday worship at my church" from time to time. But I'm working to adopt clear and specific language for a more biblical definition of worship. These days I try to invite people to "join me for Sunday services with my church."

The difference seems subtle, but the shift is important as I allow the Scriptures to broaden my understanding of worship and church. Worship is much more than music just as God's Church is far more than a building. I now refer to what we do together on Sunday mornings exclusively as a Sunday service or Sunday gathering. I rarely refer to it as worship anymore.

The same goes for the music we sing there. Instead of calling it worship, I refer to it as "worship through music" or "songs of worship."

You might roll your eyes at this point, thinking the language doesn't matter that much, but I invite you to give it a try. As you limit the way you speak about worship to its truest, biblical definition, you will also sharpen the way you *think* about worship.

When that happens, I believe you will worship better and more. And God is so good that he's worth giving your life to, not just your Sunday singing.

Do Something Different This Sunday

One Sunday morning when my wife and I were still very new to our church, we arrived to find very few cars in the parking lot and a sign taped to the front entrance.

It read, "Thank you for coming! We're sorry we missed you. Today our church family is worshipping God by loving and serving our neighbors in this community. Please visit us online for more information or come back next Sunday. God bless you!"

Truthfully, we were shocked. Here was a church—a group of Jesus followers—who were so committed to true worship that they changed their Sunday morning routine to join in a community-wide effort to serve the poor, help the elderly, care for children, and love their neighbors throughout the community.

I'm proud to say it was this church family we chose to join. And

I encourage you to do what they did. Shift your Sunday worship from time to time from gathering to sing and listen to a sermon (which are both good things, mind you) to live a life of sacrifice together in your community.

Maybe it's serving a meal at a local shelter, completing a home repair for an elderly person, or inviting your neighbor into your home for a meal and some time with your family. Maybe it's visiting a congregation of a different ethnicity to experience the way they gather on Sundays. Maybe it's slowing down long enough to be present with your family and God. The ideas are limitless.

———

If true biblical worship is a life lived sacrificed to Jesus, then it's a twenty-four hours a day, seven days a week way of being. Gathering to worship God through music, prayer, and gospel preaching is vital stuff, but it's not all there is to a life of worship. There is much more to do and much more to be gained.

And all this would be simpler if you weren't alone. That's why Rule #5 is Join the Church. You were created to worship, but you were not created to worship alone.

What if every person in your church family committed to loving and worshipping God together? And what if they defined worship as living sacrificially instead of just singing passionately? What kind of impact might God have through you and yours as you gave your lives away for others?

These are compelling questions that have powerful answers. And it's why Give Yourself Away is Rule #7.

7

GIVE YOURSELF AWAY

"Humility is not thinking less of yourself. It's thinking of yourself less."
—C.S. Lewis

Accumulation and accomplishment, as pastor and author John Mark Comer puts it, are the twin gods of Western culture.[1] Giving *anything* away—much less our very lives—often feels impossible. Almost everything we see, hear, and read in the broader culture points in the exact opposite direction of humble generosity and self-sacrifice.

Let's take just one example: advertising. Because Western culture is built on consumerism—the preoccupation with the accumulation of goods—advertising is designed to convince you to buy more stuff.

On a deeper level, it's more sinister than that. Consumerist advertising convinces you, by design, that you are not enough. And the only way to become enough is to have more than enough.

In the not-too-distant past, advertisers introduced a product then left you to decide if you needed or wanted it. Today, the same companies pitch their products much differently. They decide for you, telling you just how incomplete your life is without their product.

Their wares are no longer billed as optional items that make life better. They're sold as the necessities that make life, *life.*

Think I'm going overboard? Pay close attention to the ads on TV, in your social media feeds, and on every billboard, magazine, or internet site. They say the same thing: Buy this and you will finally be happy.

Below the surface of these messages lies the cultural belief that all joy, happiness, truth, and wisdom are found within. Do whatever you feel you need to do, buy whatever you feel you need to buy, gain whatever you feel you need to gain, to be whatever you feel you need to be.

After all, you only live once (Y.O.L.O.), and life is about *you*, so make it count. (Oh, and this product will help with that!)

It turns my stomach to write it out this way, but it's true. The overarching message of an individualistic and consumerist culture is that your needs, wants, and desires are the truest thing about life and they must be satisfied. Ads force-feed us this message all day, every day.

If you and I are not aware and on guard, the propaganda can turn our hearts and minds, convincing us that all of life is about us.

This temptation is not new. It's been this way a very, very long time. The Fall—hauntingly summarized in the third chapter of Genesis—is the human tendency to rebel against our Creator and hoist the God-mantle onto our own shoulders. The mantle doesn't fit, though we believe it should and are dead set to prove it.

Unfortunately, our selfish rebellion wrecks the cosmos. Not only does sin splinter our relationship with God, it drives wedges in our relationships with one another and throws our relationship with the planet off-kilter. It's ugly, ugly stuff. Just turn on the nightly news.

What's the remedy to our selfishness? God himself, of course.

But how does he remedy us? By giving himself away and teaching us to be just like him. Self-sacrifice is more than the opposite of selfishness. It's the way in which God saved the world and it's his design for human thriving.

Giving ourselves away is the way God created us to be, and when we step into his way—even with baby steps—we discover Jesus was right when he said the key to living is giving.

The Servant King

By the end of Jesus' earthly ministry, the disciples' experience with him defied description. They'd witnessed it all. They saw bread and fish multiplied, wind and waves rebuked, and disability, dysfunction, disease, and death defeated. They heard God's voice and touched God's face.

Though they learned to expect the unexpected from Jesus, none seemed prepared for his final acts of humility. Jesus of Nazareth was proving himself to be God in the flesh—the King of kings and Lord of lords—yet he continually flipped the script. His words and actions, culminating in the cross, reversed his followers' thinking about power, privilege, and the purpose of human life.

One particularly poignant display of Jesus' way unfolded at dinnertime the night of his betrayal and arrest. The Bible tells us that the high and exalted Jesus did something very lowly. John's gospel provides the details.

> Jesus knew that the Father had given him authority over every-thing and that he had come from God and would return to God. So he got up from the table, took off his robe, wrapped a towel around his waist, and poured water into a basin. Then he began to wash the disciples' feet, drying them with the towel he had around him. (John 13:3-5)

This scene is weird for us today. We don't wash each other's feet in any scenario, much less at the start of dinner. But washing a guest's feet was common in Jesus' day.

A first-century homeowner or dinner host would designate a bowl of water, towel, and a servant to rinse, wipe clean, and dry his visitor's dirty sandal-clad feet. If he could not afford a servant, the host gave guests the opportunity to wash the day's grime from their own feet. Every guest enjoyed the refreshing and thoughtful practice.

So it was not the act of washing feet that caught the disciples off guard. It was the unimaginable fact that Jesus—God in the flesh —did the washing.

Jesus washed their feet then spoke these remarkable words:

> Do you understand what I was doing? You call me "Teacher" and "Lord," and you are right, because that's what I am. And since I, your Lord and Teacher, have washed your feet, you ought to wash each other's feet. I have given you an example to follow. Do as I have done to you. I tell you the truth, slaves are not greater than their master. Nor is the messenger more important than the one who sends the message. Now that you know these things, God will bless you for doing them. (Matthew 13:12-17)

In this act Jesus introduced his disciples to a new paradigm: one in which the first will be last, the king will be servant, and those who long to live their real lives will give their lives away. Soon after he would do the unimaginable. He humbled himself completely by dying for them—and us—on the cross.

Jesus, God the Son, gave everything for our reconciliation and salvation. If anyone knows what's gained by losing one's life and the blessing of giving, it's him. Which is why his teaching about both carries eternal weight.

The Giving Paradox

The scene in which Jesus washed his disciples' feet—including Judas, the one who betrayed him to death only a few hours later—is the real-life embodiment of two of Jesus' least popular teachings for today's individualistic and consumeristic mindsets.

The first teaching is,

> If you try to hang on to your life, you will lose it. But if you give up your life for my sake, you will save it. (Luke 9:24)

The second is,

> "It is more blessed to give than receive." (Acts 20:35)

Ugly truth be told, we are much more likely to believe the opposite of those statements. We believe hanging on to our lives is the only way to save them. After all, nobody looks out for you except, well, *you*.

And we believe it's a lot better to receive than to give. Particularly because it seems we don't have much when compared to a lot of other people. *It sure would be nice to receive a bit more before I start giving stuff away*, we think.

I get it. Every time I read Jesus' words, my inner self throws a fit like a spoiled three-year-old. Thankfully, the Spirit of the living God does what Jesus promised he would do—he points me back to Jesus.[2] He reminds me of the foot-washing scene in John 13, helping me see that life is found when I give mine away and that it is better to give than receive.

But before we can give our lives away we must think rightly about them. Before you and I can act like Christ, we must have the mentality of Christ.

Mentality First

I heard a story once of a man who'd just purchased a new car. Fresh off the showroom floor, it was a car he long saved his hard-earned money to buy.

A week later someone sideswiped his perfect new ride in the grocery store parking lot, leaving a huge dent and gnarly scratches. The sight turned his stomach, leaving him shocked and disappointed.

He took a long look at the newly damaged and defaced vehicle, sighed, glanced toward the sky and muttered, "Lord, I have no idea why you want dents and scratches in the side of your new car, but now you've got 'em." Then he pried the door open, got in, and drove home.

I don't know if the story is real, but the parable is true. I've met real people who share that humble man's mentality, and I long to be like them. Folks like this understand who really owns their life and things.

Discipleship to Jesus is giving back to him what's already his. In his first letter to the Corinthian church, the Apostle Paul wrote, "You do not belong to yourself, for God bought you with a high price."[3] As the Heidelberg Catechism affirms, our greatest hope in life and death is found in the truth that we are not our own.[4]

When I first began to write, blogger and writing coach Jeff Goins convinced me that the first step to become a writer is to think of myself as one. Until I convinced myself that I am a writer —not just someone who sometimes writes—I would never live up to my full writing potential.

The same goes for giving yourself away. When your mindset about life shifts from owner to steward, you treat your life, relationships, and possessions very differently. And you experience the freedom that comes with leaving ultimate responsibility and results to God.

If you're like me, this mentality is difficult to adopt, but we can begin to allow God to shape our mentality by asking a handful of questions and meditating on the answers found in God's Word.

Take time to consider each question below and look up each accompanying passage of Scripture. Let God continue to shift and shape your mentality through his Word.

- Who invented humanity? (Genesis 1-2, Psalm 100:3)
- Who designed and formed every stitch of every thing in our world? (Psalm 33:6-9, Job 38-41, Colossians 1:15-20)
- Who made *you*? (Psalm 139)
- Who humbly entered into his creation to redeem it? (Matthew 1:22-23, John 1:1-18, Philippians 2:5-11)
- Who loved you and all his creation so much that he endured the absolute worst of it to heal all that's broken, redeem all that's damned, and find and save all that's lost? (Isaiah 53, John 1, Colossians 1:19-22)
- Who literally died for you and for me? (John 3:16-17, Romans 5:6-11, Galatians 2:20)
- Last but not least, who is it that followers of Jesus give their lives completely to and for? (Jeremiah 10:23, John 15:4-5, Romans 12:1-2)

If your answer to any of these, much less all of them, is God, then these next questions are simple.

- To whom do you belong?
- To whom do you owe your life?
- If you belong completely to God, what role do you play in deciding what to do with yourself?

Like you, I am prone to believe the lie that I am my own. The world around me values self-expression, self-actualization, and self-empowerment and encourages me to think primarily of myself. I often give in. I think only of myself, sometimes in too lofty of terms, and sometimes in terms too lowly.

But the truth is, I am not my own. I am God's. From beginning to end, from first breath to last, I live and breathe in the world God invented with the heart, lungs, and brain *he* made.

Like the man with the new car, giving yourself away is realizing that everything you have and everything you are is not yours. It's God's, and God's alone.

Once that mentality is set, you will experience the freedom you need to actively give yourself away for God's glory, others' good, and your joy.

Activity Second

Many of us wrongly believe that what we do determines our standing before God. We're tempted to believe that we earn God's favor. But the reality is we are loved and chosen by God, full of grace, and we didn't earn what we receive from him.

Active, humble participation in God's kingdom happens when our hearts and minds are rooted in the truth of that good news.

With that in mind, what does it look like to give yourself away? You live generously, remembering that you are not your own, and you allow God's Spirit to bear his kind of fruit in your life. Let's look at both now.

Generous Living

How have you experienced generosity lately? Here's how I've experienced it in the few weeks leading up to the writing of this chapter:

- A friend helped me improve the quality of my work.
- My wife listened for a long time as I rambled on about one of my hobbies.

- A colleague bought my lunch.
- Friends spent a day in prayer for me.
- My dad taught me how to use a tool.
- A mentor took my phone call and patiently answered a barrage of questions.
- My brother hosted my family at his home.
- I got a simple but timely text that read, "How are you?"

The word "generosity" or "give" most often reminds us of money. And writing checks can certainly fall in the generosity category. Jesus talked about money routinely, and he wants us to share it liberally.

But generosity is far more than just giving money.

Generous people give kindness, time, attention, and love. Generosity leads us to hold a hand, give a hug, share a smile. It gets the grass cut, packs boxes, provides a ride, buys groceries, asks questions, solves problems, or starts over.

Generous people fight for justice, forgive faults, and tell the truth. Generosity is being joyful and gentle, celebrating and mourning, giving *and* receiving.

The generous are more aware of others than themselves, and they offer whatever they have to whomever they're with whenever it's needed.

I believe, therefore, that generosity is at the core of the Christian life. Here's why: Jesus (surprise, surprise), and the fruit of his Spirit.

Join me in a thought experiment and I'll show you what I mean. Read the following passage of Scripture with this question in mind: *What does this passage have to do with generosity?*

Though he was God, he did not think of equality with God as something to cling to. Instead, he gave up his divine privileges; he took the humble position of a slave and was born as a human being. When he appeared in human form, he humbled himself in obedience to God and died a criminal's death on a cross. (Philippians 2:6-8)

Can you think of a more remarkable display of generosity? I can't because I don't believe there is one.

Remember, the one Paul wrote of is *God*—as in the being who tells the sun to heat a specific planet in a specific solar system for a specific purpose. He's the God who not only *invented* us, but also loves, sustains, enjoys, and engages us.

He made us from scratch—along with every pinch and parcel of the world we inhabit—*by the sound of his voice!*[5]

It's *that* God that Paul had in mind when he wrote, "Though he was God."

Though he was God he made himself nothing.[6] *Nothing.* He gave up his divine privileges and became a servant. This is like a human being making himself a twig. Or a housefly. Or an individual atom in the fiber of the dirty carpet under your feet.

And this great God did so to save everything that matters from its own self-destruction.

It's there, then, that we find a kind of self-giving that's the first and perfect definition of generosity. Now let's take a peek at the second.

Generous Fruit

The Bible says this in Galatians 5:22-23:

The Holy Spirit produces this kind of fruit in our lives: love, joy, peace, patience, kindness, goodness, faithfulness, gentleness, and self-control. There is no law against these things!

Repeat the previous exercise. Read those two verses again and ask how they relate to generosity.

Here's what I see: A life characterized by love, joy, peace, patience, kindness, goodness, faithfulness, gentleness, and self-control is a *very* generous one. Each spiritual fruit is its own brand of generosity.

Love is the most generous of all spiritual fruit. God is love,[7] and as recipients of his unremitting love, we have infinite value—even when we don't deserve it. Love then, is the generosity of value. We are generous when, like God, we value and love all people, even our enemies.[8] Love values all people because God created us in his image,[9] and Jesus sacrificially died for us all.[10] Love for others is the heart and soul of generosity.

Joy is the generosity of optimism and contentment, gratitude and hope. Joy comes from trusting God so deeply that we can thank him in all circumstances, and it affords us the ability to enjoy and share genuine optimism and contentment with those around us.

Peace is the generosity of confidence and rest. It's the quiet assurance that all will be well, even when it doesn't seem so, and the generosity of stability and support when another's world goes sideways.

Patience is the generosity of time and forgiveness. Patience gives focused attention to others and allowance for faults realizing everyone progresses in holiness slowly.

Kindness is the generosity of decency. Kindness considers others at all times.

Goodness is the generous fight against evil. Goodness lives the way we were meant to live with others, doing what's right, positive, productive, and pure.

Faithfulness is the generosity of evangelism. Faithfulness points others to the God who loves them and gave everything to bring them into his family. Faithfulness is the full commitment to God that invites everyone to experience him for themselves through what we say and do.

Gentleness is the generosity of care. Gentleness eliminates harshness so people can work together, be together, and walk together. It realizes everyone is fragile, wounded, and precious and generously allows them to be so.

Self-control is the generosity of restraint. Self-control intentionally and righteously holds back. It allows us to release our best and restrain our worst. It limits the rash and impetuous, and pours out the good and generous.

———

God is so generous that he produces this generous fruit in all who surrender to him. We don't drum these up for him. He delivers them to us and through us.

God loves you and me so much that he generously gives himself away so we are empowered to give ourselves away to him for others. The fruit of his indwelling Spirit is generosity at its best.

What Happens if You Don't Give Yourself Away?

If you don't give yourself away to God and, therefore, to others, you may still become quite successful, connected, reputable, confident, and intelligent. In other words, giving yourself away is no prerequisite for the American ideal of success. In many ways, it's the opposite.

But the cliché is true: No-one on their death bed wishes they were wealthier, more selfish, or isolated. The deathbed musings of the greedy, arrogant, and lonely are regretful and unsatisfied. Those of the generous, humble, and loved are quite different.

Any body of water that has no outlet becomes stagnant, then toxic. The key to a body of water being a healthy ecosystem is an outlet. The water must come in to bring fresh life, and it must go out to maintain health and vitality.

We humans are no different.

Without outlets to give yourself away, you won't tap into the true design of the Creator. Instead, you will be thwarted in your attempt to experience the life God created.

Sure, you might experience the American Western post-Enlightenment vision of autonomy and success, but the spiritual life—the true life—within you will grow stagnant and even toxic.

What Happens if You Do Give Yourself Away?

Jesus once stood among a crowd and declared,

> Anyone who is thirsty may come to me! Anyone who believes in me may come and drink! For the Scriptures declare, "Rivers of living water will flow from his heart." (John 7:37-38)

We are designed to receive living water—the Spirit of God—from Jesus, then allow him to produce his spiritual fruit within us.

Notice there's an inlet and an outlet. We come to Jesus in faith to drink (inlet), and "living water"—or the Spirit of God—pours out of him, through us, to others (outlet).

This was God's design for his people from day one. In Genesis 12, God called Abram (later renamed Abraham), and this is what he said:

> Leave your native country, your relatives, and your father's family, and go to the land that I will show you. I will make you into a great nation. *I will bless you* and make you famous, and *you will be a blessing to others*. I will bless those who bless you and curse those who treat you with contempt. All the families on earth will be blessed through you. (Genesis 12:1-3)

Abram—and later all the Jewish people—received God's blessing (inlet) *so that* they could bless all the nations (outlet).

You see, friend, God's love and blessing are for you, but they are *never* intended to end with you. Every follower of Jesus is a conduit, a vehicle, a vessel by which God delivers his love and blessing to others. The ministry of the church is a multiplication ministry for one reason: God desires to reach all people and deputizes us as his ambassadors in that cause.[11]

When you give your life away, you reach your full potential as a child of the King, chosen and called to receive his grace and goodness and then to extend his grace and goodness to others on his behalf.

How I Practice Rule #7

When it comes to practical ways to give yourself away, there are many. In her classic book, *The Spiritual Disciplines Handbook,* Adele Calhoun writes about two in particular that line up with the chapter headings above, "Mentality First" and "Activity Second." I have learned much from Calhoun's handbook, and these two practices continue to be my starting point for giving myself away.

Mentality

My first step in giving myself away is to remember what God says about the purpose of life, and nothing rightly shapes my mentality like a slow reading of the Word of God.

On this particular Rule, I take Calhoun's recommendation to meditate on the story of the Good Samaritan in Luke 10:25-37. I recommend the same to you.

In one of your times of space dedicated to listening to Jesus, slowly and prayerfully read the full passage. Pay close attention to what happens and who helps whom. Ask the Holy Spirit to reveal the character with whom your life is currently most aligned. This is challenging but fruitful work.

Are you more like the priest, the Levite, the Good Samaritan, or the innkeeper? Or perhaps the victim or even the robbers? Allow

God to lead you to see, think, and become like the Good Samaritan who recognizes another's need and resolves to meet it.

When it comes to my mentality, nothing shapes it like listening to Jesus by reading his Word slowly.

Activity

Borrowing from Calhoun again: "Every morning for the next two weeks ask your spouse, roommate or a colleague, 'What can I do for you today?' Then do it."[12] The simplicity of this practice is refreshing. The execution of it is game-changing.

I regularly ask my wife or friends how I can help. The truth is, I don't always want to help. But each time I release myself to God, recognize that I serve him when I serve others, and lend a hand, the Spirit of God fills me with purpose and meaning. No lie. It happens *every time* because this is what God built me for. He built you this way, too.

By the way, in the middle of writing the second draft of this very section, my phone rang. You can't make this stuff up.

It was my good friend Billy with the ever-dreaded question on his lips. "Hey man," he said, "are you busy right now?"

I was. But thankfully—on this occasion—the Spirit of God in me answered before my flesh could. "I'm writing," I said, "but do you need anything? I'm happy to help."

Sure enough, his wife's car broke down on the opposite side of town from him, and she and their son needed help. So I put aside the tasks I wanted to accomplish, jumped in my truck, and gave myself away.

Does that make me Mother Teresa? Hardly. But I experienced God's kingdom as I gave myself away doing what he built us to do. And it was worth every minute.

Later I got back to writing this chapter so I could challenge you to do the same thing. You won't regret it.

Warning: Too Much of a Good Thing

The one item missing in this chapter is a warning. In our inextinguishable ability to twist all of God's good things into unhelpful and even harmful things, we can take giving ourselves away too far.

The majority of us are *not* in danger of doing this, but some are. Those for whom giving oneself away is an addiction, idolatry, or the tragic result of victimization—this warning is for you.

The biblical idea of giving yourself away, of the last being first, is *not*....

- *Permission to Abuse* – Giving yourself away is not giving others permission to abuse you. After all, just like them, you are an image-bearer, built by God to reflect his image into the world. That gives you infinite value. Self-giving love for others is not the blithe receipt of abuse and/or neglect. Don't confuse the two.

- *Loss of Identity* – Giving yourself away is not a loss of your identity. Some of us obsess with doing things for others, and we forget that we are real people. We fail to ask for what we need and become desperately lonely as we struggle to believe that anyone—God included—is aware of us. Don't redefine Give Yourself Away into Become Nothing and Nobody.

- *Sacrifice for the Sake of Sacrifice* – Sacrifice for the sake of sacrifice is not God's intention. As mentioned above, giving yourself away can be twisted from a holy response to God to a sinful and selfish act of our own will. There's but one person who took away the sin of the world, and it's not you. His call for us to sacrifice is not for the sake of sacrifice or your reputation as one who sacrifices. It's for the sake of his kingdom coming and his will being done.

King David wrote this in Psalm 51:

Open my lips, Lord, and my mouth will declare your praise. You do not delight in sacrifice, or I would bring it; you do not take pleasure in burnt offerings. My sacrifice, O God, is a broken spirit; a broken and contrite heart you, God, will not despise. (Psalm 51:15-17)

———

Rule #7 is one of the most difficult practices of the Christian life. Everything—and I do mean *everything*—in this world resists this Rule. Western culture teaches you to think only of yourself, get as much as you can for yourself, and spend everything you have on yourself.

Adding insult to injury is our heart's pre-existing sinful bent toward narcissism. The desire to rule our lives the way God rules the world tempts us away from giving ourselves up to God.

It's counterintuitive in our secular culture and to our tarnished hearts, but your life is *made* to give away. You realize your true potential, joy, passion, purpose, and meaning when you tap into that design. It's a powerful redefinition of the very purpose of life.

Lose your life in him and you will find it. And you will be much more blessed when you give than when you receive. Those who press into the Christian way of complete surrender and generosity live richly.

In the end, to Give Yourself Away is to love. Love God, love others, and love yourself. Now, to take the next step on your journey, it's crucial we talk about that beautiful four-letter word. Rule #8 is Redefine Love, and the practice will open yet another door to living your real life.

8

REDEFINE LOVE

"God's love is not a pampering love. God's love is a perfecting love...His love is a transforming love."
—James MacDonald

How many times have you made statements like these?

- I love Christmas.
- I love a good thunderstorm.
- I love my wife.
- I love _____ (insert your favorite Netflix series here).
- I love Mom's homemade enchiladas.
- I love my children.
- I love donuts.

Sometimes donuts top my list. Don't tell my wife.

What about you? Who and what do you "love"?

Love is, by far, the world's best four-letter word. But because it signifies a varying level of affection for a vast variety of things, it's true meaning gets lost in translation.

I mean, do you really feel as strongly about a sugar-covered pastry as you do your spouse or child? I doubt it. But that's the way it is with the word "love." It's ubiquity muddles its meaning, as does our current cultural milieu.

American Love

Rugged American individualism negatively shapes our definition of love. It makes love subjective and renders us unable to receive healthy and necessary forms of love like instruction, correction, and accountability.

Some aspects of American individualism are positive. For example, it's congruent with the biblical fact that every person is unique, special, and individually crafted by God. And autonomy and freedom—if rightly defined and appropriately prioritized—contribute to human flourishing.

But Westerners created a world so individualistic that each man and woman is continuously tempted to consider himself or herself the very center of that world. Individuals driven by individual concerns in an individualized culture view everything through an individualistic lens.

In any culture where autonomy becomes religion and freedom becomes license, the self becomes god. And what does that do to the definition of love? It renders it completely subjective.

If unchecked, this leads to three hundred and fifty million individuals (in the U.S. alone) expecting everyone else to honor their personal version of love. And if their personalized version of love is not honored, they will feel *un*-loved.

This narcissistic definition of love is the natural byproduct of individuals holding individualism as the highest good, and it blinds us to true, biblical expressions of love.

Yet God's love—which originates in him, wholly outside of us

—is a force that convicts and changes, shapes and sharpens. God's love refuses to leave us how we are because we are not yet all we can be.

This is why we must rely on an accurate definition and clear pictures of love as God designed it. As always, we are helped here by the retelling of a personal encounter with Jesus.

Not So Rich

Jesus and his closest followers had embarked on the trek to Jerusalem for Jesus' humanity-saving sacrifice. Along the way, a wealthy man ran up to Jesus, dropped to his knees in the dirt, and asked, "Good Teacher, what must I do to inherit eternal life?"[1]

At first glance, this is an evangelist's *dream*. Jesus' reputation preceded him, and the man came, desperate for good news about eternal life. But instead of keeping it simple, telling the man to "believe in me and you will have eternal life,"[2] Jesus reminded him of the Ten Commandments.

The man's response was straightforward. He said, "Teacher, I've obeyed all these commandments since I was young."[3] It's hard to know if the man's self-evaluation was true and humble or inaccurate and prideful.

Regardless, "Jesus felt genuine love for him,"[4] and his response displayed an aspect of love many of us have forgotten.

But before we unpack Jesus' picture of love, we need a quick Bible lesson. Unlike twenty-first century English, ancient Koine Greek (the language in which your New Testament was originally composed) had distinct words for various kinds of love. Here is a helpful rundown of three words used in the New Testament.

- *Storge*: This Koine Greek word denotes a familial connection. This is the love you feel for relatives or others brought together by a common bond. A child's love and appreciation for good parents is *storge*.

- *Philia*: Often referred to as "brotherly love," *philia* is the deep connection between friends who share values, interests, and participate in activities together. The love of true friendship is *philia*.
- *Agape*: The New Testament uses the word *agape* for the love that originates in God. It's unconditional, altruistic, and centered in true moral goodwill, not simple attraction or temporary affection. This is love given regardless of reward or reciprocation. Jesus' death on the cross for you and me perfectly embodies God's *agape* love for us.[5]

These biblical definitions of love are important to know when looking at Jesus' next words to the rich young man, which fail to square with our current cultural definition and expectation of love. Jesus' words align with the heart of God in pure *agape* love.

> Looking at the man, Jesus felt genuine love for him. "There is still one thing you haven't done," he told him. "Go and sell all your possessions and give the money to the poor, and you will have treasure in heaven. Then come, follow me." (Mark 10:21)

Jesus' "genuine love" for the man in question is *agape* love. Jesus loved him so purely that he refused to allow anything in the man's life to stand in the way of his experience of God, eternal life, and discipleship. Which means Jesus had to tell him about the specific thing that stood between a "good" life and a whole one.

The text tells us the man heard Jesus' words, and his "face fell, and he went away sad, for he had many possessions."[6]

Jesus left it there. He did not change his mind or his approach. He did not coddle the man or offer words of pity or comfort.

Did the man eventually lay down his idol of wealth and come follow Jesus? Only God knows the end of that story. Yet the Bible is clear: Jesus "genuinely loved" this man. And no one is capable of a purer love for humanity than the One who created and died for us.

This loving interaction stands in stark opposition to our cultural definition of love, in which approval and endorsement of others' behaviors and the kid-glove handling of each other's emotions rules the day. Jesus' love was (and is) above and beyond that kind of foolishness.

Jesus' love is so deep that it refuses to allow us to give our lives to the things that take life away. He has, does, and will confront our idolatry for our sake, for life's sake, for love's sake.

The God of Love and the Love of God

The book of 1 John includes a passage about God and love. I encourage you to grab your Bible and read it carefully now. You can find it in 1 John 4:7-20.

Consider what the passage communicates about the nature of God and therefore the actions of Jesus. Keep in mind that every instance of the word "love" in these verses is *agape*.

The heart of it is a three-word sentence: "God is love."[7] It's difficult to overstate the importance of these three words, yet it's easy to manipulate them.

It's not that we understand God because we know what love is; we understand love because we know who God is.

The great temptation is to define God by our definition of love rather than changing our definition of love to match the character, action, and person of God.

Defining love on our own, then viewing God through that definition, is the default practice of the growing number of "Nones"—those who claim to hold spiritual beliefs but no religious association. It's the operating system of emotionalists, those who believe their feelings provide the source of truth.

When someone says, "If you don't agree with me or approve of my lifestyle then you can't love me," that's someone who believes love is god, not God is love.

However, the person who defines love by God submits his or her understanding of what love is and how it operates in the world to who God is and how he operates in the world.

It's why 1 John 4 includes this list of truths:

- Anyone who loves is a child of God and knows God.[8]
- If we love each other, God lives in us. [9]
- As we live in God, our love grows more perfect.[10]

The passage makes claims about *who God is,* not just what God does.

God isn't just a lover. He *is* love.

God doesn't just do things that are loving. He *is* love.

John's description of God and love are not descriptions of two different things. Yes, love is an action, and it's something God does. But it's an action that flows out of his literal being, his identity.

God *is* love.

Here is why this matters—don't miss it: Because God is love, everything God does and says is loving.

One more time for emphasis: *Because God* is *love, everything God does and says* is *loving.*

And that, my friend, is the key to redefining love.

Let's take some time now to explore some of the most well-known sayings of God and discover just how loving they are.

Love is Restriction

One thing is clear about love in twenty-first century America: Restriction of any kind has nothing to do with it. Autonomy, independence, license, entitlement, and unrestricted permission to behave in any way one deems fit undergirds our cultural psyche.

"If you love me," the thought goes, "then you must not restrict my 'freedom.' You will permit and endorse my behavior. If, that is, you really love me."

But there's a problem. In the words of Jeremiah the prophet, "The heart is deceitful above all things, and desperately sick; who can understand it?"[11]

Not much has changed in two and a half millennia. Our hearts alone can't be trusted to define love or act lovingly, and they still don't know intuitively what true freedom is or how to handle independence.

Therefore, throughout the Bible, God places restrictions on his community of people and advises they stick to them for the benefit of all. The most obvious example is the Ten Commandments.

Restriction repulses many a twenty-first century mind, but I challenge you to read the Ten Commandments in Exodus 20 or Deuteronomy 5 with this question in mind: What would society be like if every person in it obeyed these commands?

Spoiler alert: It would be utopia.

God's commands are so good for us that if we obeyed just these ten, we would experience the good life as never before.

With that in mind, let's look at how these rules and restrictions actually display God's love and unveil his proven pathway to genuine joy and freedom for us all.

1. You must not have any other god but me.

This is the most loving of all God's commands. It doesn't take much intellectual horsepower to understand why.

If the God of the Bible is the ultimate being, the one true source of life, the inventor and sustainer of all humankind and the very genesis of love itself, it makes sense to devote yourself to him.

Here's a simple thought experiment. If all other "gods" are imposters—cheap, man-made substitutes for the real thing—then an order from the Real Deal to worship only the Real Deal is a loving gift.

If your child has access to gasoline, bleach, and water, and you command her to only drink the water, is your restriction loving or unloving?

2. You must not make for yourself an idol of any kind.

This command echoes the first. To "make for yourself an idol" is to devote your life to anything that's not God.

God is deeply concerned about and dedicated to your welfare. The last verse of this command proves it. "I lavish unfailing love for a thousand generations on those who love me and obey my commands."[12]

Devoting yourself to any other person, place, or thing prevents you from centering your affection and obedience on God, which robs you of the glorious opportunity to experience his lavish love.

3. You must not misuse the name of the Lord your God.

Many of us as kids dared not utter the words "Oh my God." Because if Grandma heard, she just might cut out your tongue. But reducing this command to a prohibition on cursing is far too shallow for the magnitude of God.

God's third command has more to do with the atrocities of 9/11 than a dirty mouth. Why? Because flying planes into buildings to honor God does no such thing. It's a disgraceful affront to God and a gross misuse of his name.

Similarly, controlling and manipulating others in the name of God is a shameful misuse of his name.

Cursing, judging, and hating people created in his image is a gross misuse of his name.

Giving yourself permission to act selfishly and impetuously while claiming God "told me to do it" is a gross misuse of his name.

God's intention behind this command is to prevent folks from doing something in his name that does not align with his nature.

God's love for us and others is on full display when he commands us to leave his name out of our unloving deeds.

4. Remember to observe the Sabbath day by keeping it holy.

God has known all along what health professionals regularly talk about: Human beings need rest. Doctors remind us to get eight hours of sleep, but we're too tired to listen. Sociologists tell us a sixty-hour work week is *less* productive than a forty-hour one, but we're too busy to pay attention.

God made humans to thrive when we sleep through the night, take breaks from work, and create margin in our lives. He also made us to thrive when we devote every day—working and resting —to him[13] (see the first Commandment above).

It's this thriving that God is concerned with when he lovingly calls his people to observe a Sabbath day and keep it holy. He built us to routinely rest and refuel with him and others, remember and thank him for his goodness, and relax into the gracious reality that everything does not depend on us. This is God's original command to fight for space.

This chapter's scope is too limited to fully unpack what observing the Sabbath looks like today, but I encourage you to dig into some resources[14] on your own and discover the love of God behind this command.

5. Honor your father and mother.

Like remembering the Sabbath, this command deserves a more thorough treatment than what is possible here, but a couple of points are worth making.

This command seems particularly sticky given the continued disintegration of God's family order, the tragedy of broken families, and the number of us who were parented by mothers and/or fathers we feel do not deserve our respect.

But the value of honoring one's father and mother is not based on the changing current of culture or the bad behavior of parents. It's rooted in the perfect design of God.

God designed the family to be the foundation of every home, community, and society. When we revere God by respecting our parents, we participate in his created order and help the world work as it should. And when others readily accept some alternative family design that is not of God, our efforts to honor our parents provide healthy resistance to the world's broken way.

That honors God and is loving for all.

6. You must not murder.

Now we're getting to the easy ones! Do I even need to explain why this restriction is rooted in love? Probably not, but here's an explanation anyway.

Human beings are God's most treasured creation, and we are created in his image.[15] Extinguishing another human life is an affront to God because it destroys a representative of him in the world. The ending of human life is a rejection of God himself.

Even given our place as God's most beloved creation, we are not God. We cannot and therefore should not determine when another precious human dies. That's God's role, not ours.

God's order not to murder is the most basic of loving restrictions.

7. You must not commit adultery.

It's unfortunate that the goodness of this restriction must be explained, but such is the reality in our emotion-based, narcissistic society. Adultery, no matter how you look at it, is destructive and unloving.

Indulgence may feel like love in the moment, but it's an arrogant and irresponsible act with an intruder that, in the end, destroys the hope for real love and intimacy with the one whom God has given you. And when adultery leads to divorce it destroys entire families, children's emotional health and stability, and even God's witness in a needy world.

Adultery mocks God's plan for marriage, and it prevents others from seeing God's love for his Church through covenant-keeping couples. Pursuing your spouse and maintaining a marriage come hell or high water is very difficult, but it's a source of love that points to God himself.[16]

8. You must not steal.

In some ways, this command sums up the other ten. Each can be seen as a kind of theft.

Bowing to other gods steals the worship due the one true God.

Misusing his name steals the truth of God's character from people.

Murder steals human life.

Adultery steals love and intimacy from the one to whom you are married.

False testimony steals what's true and right from another.

Covetousness steals joy and contentment from yourself.

Like murder, this is a no-brainer. There's nothing loving about taking what's not yours from someone else. God restricts stealing because a society that moralizes it deteriorates into chaos. If it's unloving to steal, it's loving to restrict it.

9. You must not testify falsely against your neighbor.

In the exalted life of Jesus, love and truth are inseparable. His interaction with the rich young man, as explored above, exemplifies that.

Though lying feels expedient, practical, and even necessary at times, it diminishes love. God puts a restriction on false testimony because love thrives in truth, in the light, in what's real.

When we distort the truth, love takes a hit. We cheapen neighborly relationships. We fail to uphold the second portion of the greatest commandment—to love our neighbor as ourselves. But every time we speak truth, God's kingdom comes, his will is done, and love is known.

10. You must not covet.[17]

The command to "not covet" is particularly interesting and difficult.

Why so interesting? Because it deals with our thoughts, feelings, and desires, not just our actions.

Why so difficult? Because our cultural indoctrination of lust, greed, and materialism encourages covetousness at every turn.

You and I are taught from birth to evaluate what we have (or don't have) and compare it to what others have (or don't have). Then we are trained to long for what they have or feel pride because we have more.

Do you understand how destructive and unloving this is? When we see each other as owners of stuff rather than creations of God, we feel free to covet, steal, or withhold one another's things. It's the opposite of God's self-sacrificing, self-giving, generous, and grace-filled nature. It's the opposite of love, so God lovingly restricts it.

————

The God who is love kindly points out our problems and gives restrictive commands to spare us from dangerous traps. Life-taking traps.

Ironically, a life without restriction, discipline, and order is no life at all. God's "restrictions" free us to live the lives with him and each other that we were made to live. God's love is extended —not restrained—by his good and purposeful design for our actions.

Now, let's see how true love is discovered in intention, not just action.

Love is Intention

Have you read *1984* by George Orwell? It's a trip. Orwell imagined a government that so thoroughly propagandized, manipulated, monitored, and controlled its citizens that it could, for all intents and purposes, read everyone's minds and discern their true intentions. It's a disturbing possibility to consider.

Interestingly, Christians believe there *is* someone who can read your mind. But in stark contrast to Orwell's fictional almighty State, that someone is God. And unlike the State, he is perfect and good, unbent by sin and evil.

God "knows the thoughts of man"[18]and the depravity of our hearts, and he's not content to leave us in our crookedness. So in his famous Sermon on the Mount, Jesus addresses our intentions.

According to Jesus, love is what you think, feel, believe, and intend, not just what you do.

In his most famous speech, the Son of God affirms the Ten Commandments, but then he raises the bar.

Jesus Raises the Bar

The Old Testament law serves three purposes. It points to God's holiness, reveals our heart's sinful nature, and proves our need for a Savior.

In the Sermon on the Mount, Jesus brandishes his spiritual scalpel and begins heart surgery. He dives deeper into our depravity, divulging just how badly we need him.

Below is a portion of what he said. But be warned, his truth will lay you bare. Read these excerpts from the Sermon and try not to resist the Holy Spirit's convicting work.

> You have heard that our ancestors were told, "You must not murder. If you commit murder, you are subject to judgment." But I say, if you are even angry with someone, you are subject to judgment! If you call someone an idiot, you are in danger of being brought before the court. And if you curse someone, you are in danger of the fires of hell..."
>
> You have heard the commandment that says, "You must not commit adultery." But I say, anyone who even looks at a woman with lust has already committed adultery with her in his heart....
>
> You have also heard that our ancestors were told, "You must not break your vows; you must carry out the vows you make to the Lord." But I say, do not make any vows! Do not say, "By heaven!" because heaven is God's throne. And do not say, "By the earth!" because the earth is his footstool...Just say a simple, "Yes, I will," or "No, I won't." Anything beyond this is from the evil one...
>
> You have heard the law that says, "Love your neighbor" and hate your enemy. But I say, love your enemies! Pray for those who persecute you! In that way, you will be acting as true children of your Father in heaven. For he gives his sunlight to both the evil and the good, and he sends rain on the just and the unjust alike. If you love only those who love you, what reward is there for that? Even corrupt tax collectors do that much. If you are kind only to your friends, how are you different from anyone else? Even pagans do that. But you are to be perfect, even as your Father in heaven is perfect. (Matthew 5:21-22, 27-28, 33-37, 43-48)

Jesus knows that while most don't physically murder others, we slay them with our words, enact revenge in our minds, and hope for their demise in our hearts.

We stop short of adulterous affairs, but we enjoy emotional

intimacy with colleagues or exploit strangers through internet pornography.

We uphold our written contracts and long-term agreements at work, but we fail to keep our word with friends and family.

And in our polarized society, we turn those with whom we disagree into the opposition, content to deride them online or in our minds.

But *pray* for our persecutors? Hardly.

Love our enemies? Impossible.

Yet Jesus, without batting an eye, said, "You are to be perfect, even as your Father in heaven is perfect."[19] In his incisive sermon he calls us to the very highest standard of purity within and without.

Connecting the Dots

What does this have to do with redefining love? Let me answer you this way...

The heart is the engine that drives our actions, and the God who created us cares about who we are, not just about what we do.

Matthew recorded these words of Jesus to some members of the religious elite of his day:

A tree is identified by its fruit. If a tree is good, its fruit will be good. If a tree is bad, its fruit will be bad. You brood of snakes! How could evil men like you speak what is good and right? For whatever is in your heart determines what you say. A good person produces good things from the treasury of a good heart, and an evil person produces evil things from the treasury of an evil heart. (Matthew 12:33-35)

With Jesus' words in mind, let me ask you a question: Are you familiar with behaviorism? Behaviorism is the belief that only our actions matter. "Don't worry about controlling your thoughts or emotions or feelings or beliefs," the behaviorist says, "just keep your actions reined in, and all will be well."

It's a nice idea, but it doesn't work for very long. At some point —at *many* points—what is harbored in our hearts gets lived out in our lives.

Love in a Christian's life starts with the regeneration of his heart. That's a profound work of God that the Holy Spirit performs in lives all over the world every day.

People can fool—and be fooled by—one another, but God sees through what we do and reads our hearts like an open book.

And it's inside *there* that his unbelievable love does unbeatable work. It's inside *there* that his reforming love transforms.

True love—love redefined—is birthed inside us by a God who cares about our intentions and the actions born out of them.

Loving the Hard Way

A few years back a man I know was poised to make a selfish and marriage-ending decision. He was so consumed with his own discomfort that he saw no path forward. Fortunately, some of his friends did.

One night, the friends gathered for their weekly get-together, and the man announced his intention to divorce his wife. His decision was made.

He hoped to receive what other friends and family gave: understanding nods, encouraging sentiments, and even words of endorsement and prayers for a new beginning.

On this night, he had no such luck. These faithful men pointed him to Scripture, gently but firmly clarified his selfish motives, and stood determined to turn him back to God and back to his wife. They told him to do the hard thing, the godly thing, the non-emotion-based thing. They told him to do the difficult but loving thing.

I believe, like Jesus and the rich young man, this man's friends loved him to the end. The conversation was excruciating. He was surprised, upset, and hurt because he *felt* betrayed. But the truth was his friends did *not* turn on him. Rather, they turned *to* him and attempted to turn him toward God.

The group could see what he could not. They saw what stood in his way to God's best for him, and it would have been unloving to pat him on the back, say "it's going to be alright," and then watch him destroy the marriage God wanted to save.

In the mind of God, those true friends demonstrated love by asking the hard questions and probing below the surface in an attempt to preserve their marriage. It was loving to hold up a higher standard without cowering to the momentary emotion.

Godly love is well rounded. It includes acceptance and encouragement, care and devotion, but it also includes good intentions, anger at what's bad and wrong, and discipline when needed.

To love one another is going to require us to sometimes do counter-cultural and personally uncomfortable things. And *to be loved* requires us to ask for, hear, and receive counter-cultural and personally uncomfortable things.

But if we learn anything from Jesus' interaction with the rich young man, it's that God is more interested in our thriving than in our comfort, in our ultimate perfection than in our temporary pleasure.

What Happens if You Don't Redefine Love?

Love according to Western culture's definition is like fast food. It satisfies hunger for a moment, but over time it ruins those who digest a steady diet of it. In the moment, it tastes so good, yet it's a deceptively dangerous way to eat.

Subscribe to a definition of love that's centered on your personal wants, and you will experience the pleasure of self-gratification. After all, selfishness *is* pleasurable. That's the point of it!

But it's deceptively dangerous to your soul. It leaves you parched, unsatisfied, and starving for more of what's real and healthy.

If you don't allow the God who is love to redefine love for you according to his character, three bad things happen: You stagnate, you self-delude, and worst of all, you won't know God.

First, without a godly definition of love, you will stagnate. Love is designed to move us and grow us and make us more like Jesus. It woos and wins us from our current, restricted ways of thinking and being. Live by a cultural definition of love and you will stay in one spot, never growing or maturing.

Second is self-delusion. Continue to believe what culture teaches about love—that you are the center of the universe and those who love you affirm your self-centered ideas and decisions— and you will create a false, self-deluded world that will leave you exhausted and alone. Exhaustion comes as you constantly strive to maintain a subjective reality, bending objective reality (including all your relationships) to your will. And you'll end up alone because loneliness is the natural byproduct of this sequence. In the end, all narcissists end up alone.

Third and worst of all, you won't know God. 1 John 4 is clear: "Anyone who loves is a child of God and knows God. But *anyone who does not love does not know God*, for God is love."[20] Those who know God and love like him, are his. Those that don't, aren't. And there's no bigger mistake in life than to choose a way of life and a definition of love that disconnects you from God.

What Happens if You Do Redefine Love?

The most satisfied and secure, compelling and confident, attractive and authentic people are those who understand God's true definition of love and live it out by his power daily. They may not be the most famous or the richest, but they are the most complete and joy filled.

If holding to a secular definition of love thwarts your ability to become better, then holding to God's definition allows you to mature by leaps and bounds. Love like God, and you become like him. And that's the goal.[21]

But that goal is attainable only when we see our need for spiritual refinement rather than egocentric adulation and we accept true love as a tool to sharpen and shape us.

Proverbs 17:3 reminds us that God "tests the heart" like "fire tests the purity of silver and gold." And Jesus said that God prunes his true disciples, cutting away that which is unnecessary and unfruitful.[22]

True love refuses to leave us the same. It makes us better if we understand it and submit to the ultimate lover.

How I Practice Rule #8

I once met a preacher with a powerful practice. Every Sunday he asked three trusted friends to evaluate his sermon and give him honest feedback and criticism.

He invited one friend to listen theologically and provide critical feedback about the biblical accuracy of his sermons.

He invited another to grade his sermon on how accessible and relatable it was for his congregants.

Last, he invited a friend to assess whether or not he accurately evaluated and diagnosed the culture's challenges to Christianity and the gospel's answer to those challenges.

The preacher's requests alone are brilliant. But what stands out to me is his desire. The man so deeply desired to grow as a preacher that he asked qualified listeners for constructive criticism. He boldly faced his weaknesses and failures as a communicator so he could become a *better* one.

That's brave stuff. Ninety percent of people hate public speaking altogether, much less being graded on it by their peers! I've adopted his practice for my own preaching and writing, and I'm a better communicator for it.

More importantly, however, is adopting the practice of inviting trusted others to give constructive feedback about weaknesses and failures in our lives. I've made a habit of asking people I trust to tell me the truth about my relationships and leadership so I can mature in those areas too.

I've asked my wife to gently help me see areas for improvement as a husband and a father.

I've asked friends to call me out on inconsistencies in my speech and behavior so I can grow in integrity.

I've asked colleagues to help me communicate more clearly and compassionately so I can lead better and more humbly.

Their constructive feedback is never fun to receive, but it is so valuable that I want—and need—to receive it. God uses their honest and loving observations to help me become more like him rather than leaving me as I am. And I'll take that kind of love any day of the week.

For those of you who have been criticized far too often by parents, peers, or partners, this feels dangerous. But negative, harsh, or personal criticism is not what we're after here.

The intent is to give thoughtful Christian friends permission to help us grow by identifying our spiritual blind spots. We don't need a parent or a Savior; we already have those. What we need are close friends in the faith who will sharpen us by directing us to the way of Jesus again and again.

Ask God whom he wants you to invite into this process, then listen closely for his response. It might not be who you think at first. Talk with God about it and see whom he leads you to, then invite them to read this chapter with you and talk about it.

The goal is simple. Ask them to help you see the places in which you are spiritually weak. Be open to feedback, relying on Jesus, Scripture, the Holy Spirit, and your loving friends to shape you and prune you for God's glory, others' good, and your joy.

———

Living this Rule is not easy. It's a way of thinking about, seeing, and experiencing love that directly opposes the flood of messaging you receive on a daily basis. Contrary to what you are told, love is not about you. Love is not self-determined, self-centered, and self-directed.

Love is a gift from God that when properly understood and defined frees us to be shaped by him into the man or woman he desires us to be. And if we don't allow our addiction to pleasure and personal preference to throw up roadblocks, God has more in store than we previously imagined. But we must work diligently to redefine—to *righteously* define—love.

While you are not the centerpiece of God's creation, you do matter immensely to God, to others, and to the world. So, just as there are Rules for Life with God and Rules for Life with Others, there are also Rules for Life with yourself. They are Rules #9, #10, #11, and #12 and they make up Part Three of *12 Rules for a Christian Life.*

PART III

RULES FOR LIFE WITH YOURSELF

The most important commandment is this: "...You must love the Lord your God with all your heart, all your soul, all your mind, and all your strength."

The second is equally important: "Love your neighbor *as yourself*." No other commandment is greater than these."

— Jesus (Mark 12:29-31)

9

REMEMBER WHO YOU ARE

"The Bible says that our real problem is that every one of us is building our identity on something besides Jesus."
—Timothy Keller

Figuring out who you are, and fully living into it, is no simple feat. It requires a serious dose of observation, insight, and perseverance to parse the cacophony of voices constantly telling you what to do and who to be. Crowds of people expect—and sometimes demand —different things. For example...

- Parents may expect you to follow in their footsteps, always be available, or participate in family dysfunction.
- Friends may expect you to agree with their choices, go where they go, and do what they do.
- Bosses may demand your availability, enthusiasm, and attentiveness morning, noon, and night (including weekends and holidays).

- The wealthy and famous demand you listen to their opinions and buy into their worldview.
- Politicians expect you to be as outraged and self-righteous as they are.
- Social media demands your attention, requiring you to always be turned on, conspicuous, and interested in the drivel others post.

And worst of all, we expect ourselves to be perfect. We are, as they say, our own worst critics.

But don't be fooled; most of those critical voices don't have a God-like inflection. Even the voice of your inner critic is too often trained to mimic the cultural critics who constantly say you are not living the life you were meant to live because you are not the person you are supposed to be.

They want you to be you, but only according to their definitions and desires. Thankfully, God has something to say about who you are too.

You Be You

I believe that the God who made you wants you to know, remember, and become exactly who he made you to be.

But for that to be a good thing, we must rigorously scrutinize the oft-used phrases "you be you" or "be yourself." We must be certain about what the world means by those phrases and what God means by them. I assure you, the definitions are quite different.

What the World Means by "You Be You"

In nearly every chapter of this book, I've mentioned the prevailing cultural influence in America and the West: individualism. It's an idol we must name.

Individualism is defined as "the habit or principle of being independent and self-reliant." An individualistic culture places personal autonomy and individual rights at the very top of its value system.

In Western culture, then, to "be yourself" means you define your own identity. This paradigm preaches that your interests and desires are paramount, and it's up to you to determine your identity and direct your purpose.

"You be you" really means "you create you" then live as boldly and "authentically" into that creation as possible.

It should come as no surprise that God views this kind of self-definition and identity building very differently.

What God Means by "You Be You"

The very first sentence of the Bible identifies God as Creator,[1] and the entire biblical text affirms that assertion. God imagined, invented, and breathes life into every human on the planet. He made us: cell and organ, soul and mind, fully male and female. And he desires for everyone to become their true self and live their best life according to his good design.

But God allows you and me, if we so choose, to *not* be who he made us to be. The very capacity to value—and even idolize—individualism is a gift. Our freedom is a signal of his love.

But—and this is crucial—as the original designer, God has full creative authority over his design. It was not left up to you or me to dream up what it means to be human. God did that already, and his plan is perfect. The question is will we accept it.

So what God means by "you be you" is to learn who he made you to be and then work with him to become just that.

What You Mean by "You Be You"

It's important to know which of the above two definitions of "you be you" you subscribe to. These two questions will help.

Do you claim responsibility for determining who you are and what it means to be you?

Or do you submit to the God who created you, allowing him to determine who you are, what it means to be human, and what to do in this life?

It's no easy decision. The cultural voices are loud and persuasive, and our hearts are bent toward selfishness. So even if you *want* to allow God to determine who you are, it's going to be a battle. Every unredeemed influence around and within you will steer you into the individualistic, ego-centric, and self-reliant version of yourself.

But friend, there's a different message that we all need to hear. A message we need to internalize. A message we need to believe and trust.

The God who created you, knows you.

He loves you and likes you.

And he made you to be one person and live one life: you and yours.

Thankfully, if Jesus is the Lord of your life, the Spirit of God will point you in the right direction and empower you to get there —to become who you're made to be.

You Are My Beloved

In Rule #3 I wrote about Jesus' journey into the desert where he was tempted. That desert experience prepared him for ministry in a powerful way. But one event prepared him even more: his baptism.

On the bank of the Jordan River, John the Baptist recognized Jesus as the "Lamb of God who takes away the sin of the world!"[2] And Jesus inaugurated his ministry the same way he calls us to: through baptism. As John the Baptist lowered Jesus into the Jordan's waters, the Holy Trinity showed up in a powerful way.

Jesus dripped with Earth's water, the Spirit descended like a dove, and the Father's voice rang out from Heaven, "You are my dearly loved Son, and you bring me great joy."[3]

What an unbelievable moment! Though it's highly unlikely the other folks nearby grasped its meaning (who would have?), I sure wish I'd been with them.

How good is God the Father that he declared his undying, eternal love for God the Son in the presence of God the Spirit at that baptismal? It was an identity-affirming and confidence-boosting, confirmation of his calling.

What the Father's words did for Jesus, they also do for us. They center us. They place us firmly within God's good story in which we are his ambassadors, heirs, and beloved sons and daughters. They help us remember who we are.

The man or woman who enters the world assured of his Father's love and joy—both heavenly and earthly—becomes a force to be reckoned with.

And though God may not replicate Jesus' Jordan River or Transfiguration moment in your life, he faithfully communicates who you are in his eternal Word. And the unchanging fact is God created you, knows you, loves you, likes you, and made you to be precisely who you are supposed to be.

And you will never live your real life—become who you are designed to become—until your head and heart are crystal clear about what God says about you.

Hold on to your heart; he has some very good things to say.

God Created You

There are over thirty-one thousand verses in the Bible, and within the first thirty we read this:

> God said, "Let us make human beings in our image, to be like us."
> ...So God created human beings in his own image. In the image of God he created them; male and female he created them... Then God looked over all he had made, and he saw that it was *very* good! (Genesis 1:26a, 27, and 31)

My mom cross-stitched a picture that still hangs in the kitchen of the home I grew up in. The image is a child reaching into a cookie jar with a caption that reads, "God made me, and he don't make no junk."

Grammar mistake aside, the quaint saying holds deep, Genesis 1-kind of truth. God made us, and everything he makes is good.

If you look back over those verses, you will see three true, real, and important statements that help us remember who we are and give us the freedom to be who God made us to be.

Let us make human beings in our image, to be like us.

The triune God of the universe—the One who calibrated the Earth's rotation, set stars ablaze, invented seasons and wind, leopards and porcupines, rose petals and coffee beans—created *you.* And he did it *willfully.*

You are no fluke. You are not the haphazard result of evolutionary progress or a meaningless amalgam of impersonal cells and randomly firing synapses. You were not accidentally discovered or evolved.

Everyone—including you—was made on purpose, through divine clarity of mind, determination, and desire.

In the image of God he created them; male and female he created them.

Of all the remarkable and miraculous things God created, only humans are created to be like him. All of it is an outpouring of his grand creativity and joy, but the only beings created to resemble, reflect, and represent him in the world are *you and me.*

Whether you are a man or a woman, young or old, single or married, working or in school, jobless or employed, athlete or artist, non-religious or religious, TV-lover or outdoor enthusiast, meat-eater or vegetarian, Democrat or Republican, you were created in the very image of God.

That's who you are. That's who you will *always* be, regardless of whether you feel it, choose to believe it, or decide to live in light of it.

Then God looked over all he made, and he saw that it was very good.

This is my favorite part. God forged the universe with explosive creativity.

On day one, God created light.

On day two, God created the chasm of space we call sky.

On day three, God created the water and ground of the Earth and all the vegetation that covers it.

On day four, God separated the day from the night then created the sun, moon, and stars.

On day five, God created the fish of the sea, and the birds of the air.

On day six, God created all the animals that roam the dry ground of his new planet.

After each act, the Bible tells us, God paused to evaluate his work and "saw it was good."

But then, at the end of that sixth day, when God's creativity reached its pinnacle and human beings were made, something different happened.

"God looked over all he had made, and he saw that it was *very* good!"[4]

All of God's creation is good, but it's not until he crowned it with humanity that he sat back, looked over it all, and declared with joy and emphasis that it was *very* good.

And the rest of God's story is clear. Though we're marred by sin, he still cherishes his beloved creation. He is committed to us. He pulls for us. He woos us and comes after us. He desires us. He *loves* us.

God.

Created.

YOU.

And he saw that *you* were very good.

God Knows You

One of the great religious confusions is the commingling of Christianity and deism.

Deism is the belief that the universe and humanity were indeed created by a god, but once completed, that god packed its bags and departed for another time and place, leaving the creation to its own devices. The god of deism cares not for its creation, ambivalent about whether it thrives or burns.

Though many professed Christians live like deism is true, the reality is that deism and Christianity have different gods. The triune God of Christianity—Father, Son, and Spirit—created *and* covenanted, designed *and* directs, invented *and* invests in his beloved creation. He spoke his creation into being and still speaks with the beings he created.

Psalm 139 beautifully narrates that truth. This precious piece of poetry reminds us that God knows humans very, very well and desires intimacy with all of us.

I encourage you to read and meditate on its opening verses with this question in mind: Is the God described in this psalm distant and detached, uncaring and uninvolved? Or is he something else?

> O Lord, you have examined my heart and know everything about me.
>> You know when I sit down or stand up.
>> You know my thoughts even when I'm far away.
>> You see me when I travel and when I rest at home.
>> You know everything I do.
>> You know what I am going to say even before I say it, Lord.
>> You go before me and follow me.
>> You place your hand of blessing on my head.
>> Such knowledge is too wonderful for me, too great for me to understand! (Psalm 139:1-6)

The psalmist continued later in the psalm with these words...

> You made all the delicate, inner parts of my body and knit me together in my mother's womb.
>> Thank you for making me so wonderfully complex!
>> Your workmanship is marvelous—how well I know it.
>> You watched me as I was being formed in utter seclusion, as I was woven together in the dark of the womb.
>> You saw me before I was born.
>> Every day of my life was recorded in your book.
>> Every moment was laid out before a single day had passed. (Psalm 139:13-16)

Even when you were in the *womb*, God was aware of, interested in, and involved with you.

He paid close and careful attention as he "formed [you] in utter seclusion" and wove you together "in the dark of the womb." Each and every moment of your life, since day one, is open to the insight and cherishing attentiveness of your heavenly Father.

A God who knows you this well is capable of deciding for himself if you are worth loving. And he thinks you are.

God Loves You

One of the primary claims Christians make is that God loves you. But let's be honest—that can be difficult to believe sometimes.

It's difficult to believe God is loving if the people who first told you about him weren't.

It's difficult to believe God loves you if you were taught that his love is contingent on perfect behavior.

It's difficult to believe God loves you if you buy into the lie that he only loves certain types of people.

It's difficult to believe God loves you if you think your sin took Jesus to the cross rather than his love.

But no matter the circumstances, and no matter if you believe it or not, God *does* love you.

I remember the exact occasion—in glorious detail—when God convinced me of his love. I'd been a disciple of Jesus for about a decade and a church-going believer for my entire life before that. I'd heard more sermons than I could count that declared God loved me, and I knew a handful of Bible verses that backed up those sermons.

But it wasn't until a night in my twenty-eighth year of life that I grasped and trusted the reality of God's love for me. For *me.*

That Sunday, I took a seat in the balcony to listen to a guest speaker at our church named Brennan Manning. He was a priest and author, and on this occasion, he was nothing less than a personal messenger from God.

I don't remember any other words he said, but at one point in the middle of his evening address, he began to say, "God loves you." He repeated that phrase while he slowly and purposefully looked around the audience. "God loves you," he said, a dozen or more times.

I don't know what anyone else experienced—perhaps nothing more than a simple, sixty-year-old man repeating the oft-spoken church words "God loves you." But what I experienced was a thin place. A place, right there in my regular balcony seat, in which the veil between Heaven and Earth was very, very thin.

"Chris," God said, "I love you."

It was Brennan's voice, but God's words.

"*I* love you," God repeated. "I *love* you. I love *you*."

And before long, I was a weeping mess. That night, God convinced me for the very first time that he really does love me. Even *me*.

Where were you when you were convinced beyond any doubt that God loves you? What did you feel? What kind of life did that true love bring you?

If the answers aren't clear on those questions, perhaps these are a better place for you to start...

Are you convinced that God loves you?

What prevents you from believing it?

If you're not certain God's love is real and true, would you want to be?

I'm here to tell you that it's true. It's unexpected, undeserved, unprecedented, and unrecognized by far too many...but it's true. We are loved because God is love. He lavishes it because it's who he is, even if—or when—we don't believe it.

But don't take my word for it. Here are God's words:

What marvelous love the Father has extended to us! Just look at it —we're called children of God! That's who we really are... Everyone who loves is born of God and experiences a relationship with God. The person who refuses to love doesn't know the first thing about God, because God *is* love—so you can't know him if you don't love. This is how God showed his love for us: God sent his only Son into the world so we might live through him. This is the kind of love we are talking about—not that we once upon a time loved God, but that he loved us and sent his Son as a sacrifice to clear away our sins and the damage they've done to our relationship with God... We know it so well, we've embraced it heart and soul, this love that comes from God... God is love. (1 John 3:1, 4:8-10, 16b-17 MSG)

The God of the universe loves you; where you are, who you are, as you are.

That doesn't mean that everything you do—every thought you have and every decision you make—is good. In fact, God is clear about that as well. You and I are in the fight of our lives against all the things that are not of God.

But when it comes to the true definition of what love is, how it works, and what it's for, God *loves* you. As Brennan Manning knew and said, "God loves you, God loves you, God loves you, God loves you, God loves you, God loves you."

God. Loves. YOU.

God Likes You

I'll never forget the sign that hung in my friend's office. On a bright green sheet of construction paper, our church's youth minister scribbled these true words: "God loves you." Then, in the bottom right-hand corner, in much smaller letters, was a set of equally true words: "But then again, God loves everyone."

Maybe you're one of those folks who grasps God's great love for you, yet you sense a "but" at the bottom right-hand corner of your heart. You can confidently sing "Jesus Loves Me" but you're simultaneously nagged by the thought, "But does he *like* me?"

If that's you, some general observations from God's Word just might help you believe he does.

The first is this: God in the flesh, Jesus of Nazareth, hung out with all sorts of people. And he seemed to have a blast doing it. Jesus' first miracle was recorded at a wedding—a wedding in which all the wine got drunk well before the dancing ended, and Jesus' mom asked him to keep it flowing so the party wouldn't stop.[5] To me, that's a picture of God enjoying his people.

Now think about the fellas Jesus chose as his first disciples. They were a motley crew. Jesus wasn't looking for cookie-cutter devotees.

Then there's Zacchaeus,[6] Nicodemus,[7] Mary Magdalene,[8] the woman at the well,[9] and a myriad of others (without even mentioning any of God's folk in the Old Testament). I'm hard-pressed to believe God loved them but didn't particularly like them.

As the Creator of humanity, God loves, enjoys, and delights in his creation's sparkling variety. And thankfully, God does not simply imply his enthusiasm about you. He makes it explicit as well.

For example, God's message of restoration and reunification through the prophet Zephaniah include these words...

> Cheer up, Zion! Don't be afraid! For the Lord your God is living among you. He is a mighty savior. He will take delight in you with gladness. With his love, he will calm all your fears. He will rejoice over you with joyful songs. (Zephaniah 3:16-17)

You hear that? God will take delight in you with gladness. Zephaniah proclaimed a future possibility that we enjoy in the present today. As a member of the new family of Jesus, you are united with God who delights in you and rejoices over you.

King David, the most significant king of Jewish history, wrote many of the psalms. One of David's psalms is a song that declares his love for God and God's deliverance of him from his enemies. Nestled in the poetry is verse 19: "He rescued me because he delights in me."[10]

Because he delights in me. It's one of my favorite clauses in the entire Bible.

Once you get your head around the idea that the men and women in the Bible are no more special than you are, you will receive David's words as truth for you too. *God delights in you.* And he acts on our behalf because of that fact.

God is not obligated to us. He doesn't have to help us, love us, or save us—much less delight in us. Yet he does.

Last but not least, the most convincing proof that God likes you is found in the Bible verses about God's friendship with people like us. Friendship, by its very nature, is when two people delight in each other.

God desires a friend-to-friend relationship with you. Here's the proof:

> This is my commandment: Love each other in the same way I have loved you. There is no greater love than to lay down one's life for one's friends. You are my friends if you do what I command. I no longer call you slaves, because a master doesn't confide in his slaves. Now you are my friends, since I have told you everything the Father told me. You didn't choose me. I chose you. (John 15:12-16a)

Jesus invites you into the same kind of close, passionate, deep, and self-giving friendship he had with his closest disciples.

Revelation 3:20 shares the simplest presentation of this invitation: "Look! I stand at the door and knock. If you hear my voice and open the door, I will come in, and we will share a meal together as friends."

There are few things more bonding—more friend-making—than sharing meals, and Jesus extends the invitation.

Abraham and Moses accepted it.[11]

Mary, Martha, and Lazarus enjoyed it.[12]

Jesus' disciples thrived in it.[13]

God delights in his children, and that delight is on full display through the pages of Scripture and in the lives men and women around this globe.

God. Likes. YOU.

Remember Who You Are

The ever-so-beautiful and important summary is this: God made you to be you, and the goodness of your life hinges on how well you remember that you are a child of God, fearfully and wonderfully made[14], known, loved, and enjoyed.

This revelation reaches full impact when we face the music of our cultural moment. Cultural expectations, social pressure, and inner desire to be people we're not overwhelm us. From ads on our computer screens and city billboards, to celebrity gossip rags and "reality" TV shows, to Christmas cards and office one-upmanship, we're bombarded with projections of lives that seem better than our own.

One of Satan's prolific lies today is that all your "friends" are better, happier, and more successful than you. His lies tempt us to fantasize about and attempt to transform ourselves.

But at the end of the day, you are a special creation of God. You're designed to glorify him by knowing, loving, and obeying him, while allowing him to lead you to be the strong, secure, confident, faith-filled, and loved one you are.

What Happens if You Don't Remember Who You Are?

In Ephesians 4, Paul describes God-given roles of leadership within his church:

> Now these are the gifts Christ gave to the church: the apostles, the prophets, the evangelists, and the pastors and teachers. Their responsibility is to equip God's people to do his work and build up the church, the body of Christ. This will continue until we all

come to such unity in our faith and knowledge of God's Son that we will be mature in the Lord, measuring up to the full and complete standard of Christ. (Ephesians 4:11-13)

In this portion of the letter, God communicates about specific roles he gives to specific people to carry out his mission through the Church. And when people gifted in those ways live out their calling, God's church grows in unity, faith, knowledge of God, and maturity in Jesus.

The Bible says,

Then we will no longer be immature like children. We won't be tossed and blown about by every wind of new teaching. We will not be influenced when people try to trick us with lies so clever they sound like the truth. (Ephesians 4:14)

This passage was written to leaders in God's first-century church, but it's instructive for us today. God designed all of us to use our God-given talents, abilities, intellect, and spiritual gifts for the sake of his kingdom.

But when we forget who we are—when we forget we are created, known, loved, and liked by God—we are prone to being tossed and blown by every wind in our cultural moment. Every new fad, new social demand, political power play, and unbiblical teaching or trend threatens to push us off the rails on which God made us to run.

There's an adage in marketing that states, "Target everybody, and you'll reach nobody." There's a parallel here. When we allow everyone else to tell us who we are, we end up being no one in particular.

We get tossed about, pushed here and there, constantly trying to be who the culture tells us to be and never feeling the rest, finding the meaning, and fulfilling the purpose for which we were specifically made. Soon that exhausting process leaves us stranded and wounded, uncertain of who we are or why we are here.

What Happens if You Do Remember Who You Are?

If, however, we allow God our Creator to focus and direct us into the specific identity he's given us, we will live to be the person he made us to be.

The people who know by faith that God made them, knows them, loves them, and likes them stand securely when the winds of cultural trends, difficult circumstances, and social pressure blow through their life. Those who remember they are children of the King live brave purpose-filled lives that accomplish things in his kingdom.

And listen to me here: I'm not talking about things that get you noticed in our fame-obsessed culture. Your fame is not the goal. *God's* fame is the goal. The growth of your personal kingdom is not the end. The growth of *God's* kingdom is the desired end. And his kingdom comes in simple yet significant, anonymous but valuable actions and ways.

Every time you tell the truth, God's kingdom comes.

Every time you introduce someone to Jesus, God's kingdom comes.

Every time we eliminate injustice, God's kingdom comes.

Every time we confess our sins and turn toward God, his kingdom comes.

Every time we speak a word of encouragement, rejoice over a redeemed life, weep over true pain and sorrow, visit the widow and prisoner, adopt an orphan or care for a child, take responsibility for each other and Earth, God's kingdom comes.

When you remember who you are, you become an active unwavering participant in the only kingdom that will last forever.

How I Practice Rule #9

This past year, I worked to recognize my limiting beliefs and to replace them with liberating truths.[15]

Limiting beliefs are the negative and untrue narratives, ideas, beliefs, or messages we unwittingly repeat about ourselves. God's enemy, Satan, happily reinforces our limiting beliefs to prevent us from remembering who we are, *whose* we are, and becoming who God intended us to become.

Liberating truths, on the other hand, are truths that align with God's Word and character, and they liberate us. They free us to remember and become who we are meant to be.

The spiritual practice for this chapter is to prayerfully identify your limiting beliefs and replace them with God's liberating truths. It's a simple process with crucial and chain-breaking power.

Here are a handful of the limiting beliefs the Lord helped me identify in my life, along with the liberating truths and Scriptures he gave me to replace them.

Limiting belief: I am not a good husband or father.

Liberating truth: God built me to lead my family, and my wife and children will respond to my leadership. (Proverbs 22:6, Ephesians 5:21-33)

Limiting belief: I don't know who I'm supposed to train up in the faith or how to do it.

Liberating truth: Disciple-making begins in my home, with my wife and children, (Luke 10:2, Proverbs 22:6) then spreads from there.

Limiting belief: I can't memorize Scripture.

Liberating truth: I remember everything I repeat. (Joshua 1:8, Psalm 1:1-2)

Limiting belief: I'm too different from my fellow co-pastors to effectively lead in ministry.

Liberating truth: God placed me on this team on purpose, and he will use our individual strengths as we work together to make disciples. (1 Corinthians 12:27)

Limiting belief: My writing isn't good enough.

Liberating truth: God told me to write, so my job is to write, using the desire and ability he gave me for maximum impact for his kingdom. (Psalm 25:12)

I encourage you to fight for space, settle into the quiet, and ask God this question: What are the limiting beliefs I believe about life and myself?

Then listen very carefully for what the Lord gives you. Your limiting belief may stem from a message your parents repeated, a misconception in your family or workplace, or a lie that you subconsciously tell yourself.

Be honest. Be brave. Write them down. After listing them, acknowledge that those limiting beliefs are lies.

Now review them one at a time, asking God to replace them with his liberating truth. And listen for the words of Scripture that he brings to mind.

If you do not know the Bible that well, listen for an idea or phrase from God. When he gives it, search for congruent ideas in the Scriptures. If you can't find them, then what you heard is not from God.

But when you *do* find what he says to you in Scripture, then you will have his Word, in black and white, to hold on to for life.

As God methodically replaces each limiting belief with his liberating truth, memorize the truth and the Scripture he identifies with it. Repeat them. Internalize them. Believe them. And be liberated by them.

––––––

Rule #9—Remember Who You Are—is critical for living your real life with God.

God created you, knows you, loves you, and likes you. You did nothing to deserve your existence or God's favor, yet you have both. But if you fail to remember it or live in the light of it, you will miss your real life.

This Rule leads us into the good news that God truly loves us and created us to be something special according to his design. But we must also face the bad news that despite our identity as the beloved children of God, the world provides stiff competition for our devotion, and we struggle to give ourselves fully to him.

The only way we will center our hearts, souls, strength, and minds on him is to combine Rule #9 and Rule #10. We must Remember Who We Are *and* we must Name Our Idols.

Read on to continue this necessary and life-giving work with me. It won't be easy. But you won't be sorry.

10

NAME YOUR IDOLS

"He is no fool who gives up what he cannot keep, to gain what he cannot lose."
—Jim Elliot

One of the inescapable truths about humanity is that all of us are built for worship. We are all designed to give our ultimate allegiance, honor, and lives to another.

In 2005, author David Foster Wallace gave the commencement address at Kenyon College. In the years since its delivery, the speech has been viewed and read online millions of times.

Wallace was not a Christian, yet he clearly understood and articulated the fact that everyone worships. In the speech he said the following:

> In the day-to day trenches of adult life, there is actually no such thing as atheism. There is no such thing as not worshipping. Everybody worships. The only choice we get is what to worship.

Human beings, he noted, are given the freedom to choose what to worship, but like a double-edged sword, that truth cuts two ways. The continuation of Wallace's thought explains the danger well.

> The compelling reason for maybe choosing some sort of god or spiritual-type thing to worship...is that pretty much anything else you worship will eat you alive.

Wallace's analysis of the worshipper's life is sobering, and he did not stop there. He fortified his statements with a handful of arresting, but true, examples.

> If you worship money and things, if they are where you tap real meaning in life, then you will never have enough, never feel you have enough. It's the truth.
>
> Worship your body and beauty and sexual allure and you will always feel ugly. And when time and age start showing, you will die a million deaths before they finally grieve you...
>
> Worship power, you will end up feeling weak and afraid, and you will need ever more power over others to numb you to your own fear.
>
> Worship your intellect, being seen as smart, you will end up feeling stupid, a fraud, always on the verge of being found out.[1]

You and I *will* worship, and anything we worship that is not God will indeed eat us alive.

But while you cannot choose *if* you will worship, God gives you the freedom to choose who or what you will worship.

Creator or Creation

On September 17, 2019, students and faculty at Union Theological Seminary in New York City confessed their sins... to plants.[2]

Under the professor's leadership and the seminary's endorsement, a number of potted plants were placed in the center of a classroom, and students confessed how they—and the human race in general—had wronged the world's greenery. And they encouraged others to follow suit.

Pictures were taken, tweets were sent,[3] and, as you might imagine, a firestorm erupted in the Christian media-sphere.

Albert Moehler, president of The Southern Baptist Theological Seminary in Louisville, Kentucky commented on his daily podcast, "If you do not worship the Creator, you will inevitably worship the creation, in one way or another. That's the primal form of idolatry."[4]

Even well-meaning Christians, like those at Union Theological Seminary, can lose sight of the Creator and begin worshiping his creation instead.

It's helpful here to return to Paul's definition of worship that we discussed in Rule #6.

> And so, dear brothers and sisters, I plead with you to give your bodies to God because of all he has done for you. Let them be a living and holy sacrifice—the kind he will find acceptable. This is truly the way to worship him. Don't copy the behavior and customs of this world, but let God transform you into a new person by changing the way you think. (Romans 12:1-2a)

Biblical worship begins by acknowledging that God himself—not anything he's made or given—is the one whom we worship. It's is giving up yourself so God, rather than the world around you, can shape and form how you think. That was as big a challenge for Jesus' first disciples as it is for his followers today.

One Not-So-Small Request

Jesus' disciples occupied a unique position as the very first of his followers, and God worked mightily through them. But just like us, that band of brothers was on a step-by-step journey with God marked by terrific highs, terrible lows, life-altering spiritual awakening, and dependence-revealing human blunders. The Gospel writers recorded it all in full color.

One of those blunder moments is included in Mark's Gospel, and the scene helps us to learn our tenth Rule for a Christian life: Name Your Idols.

Jesus led the way as he and his disciples headed toward Jerusalem for the final time, and he took a moment to remind them of his ultimate course.

> "Listen," he said, "we're going up to Jerusalem, where the Son of Man will be betrayed to the leading priests and the teachers of religious law. They will sentence him to die and hand him over to the Romans. They will mock him, spit on him, flog him with a whip, and kill him, but after three days he will rise again." (Mark 10:33-34)

Two thousand years later, hindsight helps us understand the full trajectory of Jesus' life. But those first disciples were living *in* those history-changing moments, not looking back on them. They knew he was Messiah, but they weren't always certain what that entailed.

Right after hearing Jesus articulate his true mission, James and John, two of his dearest friends and closest followers, made a bold request.

> Let one of us sit at your right and the other at your left in your glory. (Mark 10:37)

Jesus' ensuing dialogue with them makes it clear that these two self-promoters didn't fully grasp the nature of Jesus' "glory" and a disciple's participation in it.

"You don't know what you are asking," Jesus said. "Can you drink the cup I drink or be baptized with the baptism I am baptized with?"

"We can," they answered.

Jesus said to them, "You will drink the cup I drink and be baptized with the baptism I am baptized with, but to sit at my right or left is not for me to grant. These places belong to those for whom they have been prepared." (Mark 10:38-41)

Jesus' phrase "drink the cup I drink" reminds us of his prayer in the Garden of Gethsemane. There he talked with God about drinking "the cup" of human sin and suffering in order to redeem the world.

Tradition tells us that both James and John eventually did drink a similar cup. Because of their faith, James was beheaded, and John was banished and imprisoned.

But in this passage, they imagined something quite different. They idolized positions of power and influence, looking out only for themselves. They pictured themselves in an elevated status *next* to Jesus rather than resting in their relationship *with* Jesus.

Their power grab didn't go over well with the other disciples, and Jesus used it as a teaching moment.

When the ten heard about this, they became indignant with James and John. Jesus called them together and said, "You know that those who are regarded as rulers of the Gentiles lord it over them, and their high officials exercise authority over them. Not so with you. Instead, whoever wants to become great among you must be your servant, and whoever wants to be first must be slave of all. For even the Son of Man did not come to be served, but to serve, and to give his life as a ransom for many." (Mark 10:41-45)

Jesus took this opportunity to sharpen the spiritual focus of all the disciples. They would be different than the world. Bickering over position and power is a construct of human kingdoms, not of God's.

That moment was pivotal. Jesus helped James and John name their idols and invited them to reconstitute their devotion by placing it back in Jesus alone. He wants to help us do the same.

A Devotion Test

Grab a piece of paper (no, not your notes app in your smartphone...a *real* piece of paper), and get ready to write down the answers to these four questions.

Take a deep breath, take your time, and be honest. Nobody else will see your answers.

And, seriously, write them down. Trust me on this one.

- Who is the single most important person in your life?
- What's your most beloved possession?
- Which personal quality, characteristic, or accomplishment brings you the most satisfaction or pride?
- What's the one dream you most long to be fulfilled?

Got your answers written down? Good. Keep them close by. Here are my truthful answers.

- The single most important person in my life is my wife.
- My most beloved possession is my home.
- I take the most pride in the fact that I am well liked.
- The dream I most long for is to develop and lead a spiritual retreat ministry based on the way of Jesus and the Rules in this book.

Now take your pen and slowly draw a dark line through each of your answers. As you mark through each, imagine the possession, person, area of pride, and dream is taken away from you. Forever.

- ~~My wife~~
- ~~My home~~
- ~~My reputation~~
- ~~My spiritual retreat ministry~~

Finally, sit for a quiet moment. Feel the emotional pain of losing it all. Then answer these questions:

- If each of these disappeared today, would you still believe God is good?
- Would you still find him worthy of your worship and devotion?
- Would you be able to echo the words of Job when he lost everything? He cried out, "The Lord gave me what I had, and the Lord has taken it away. Praise the name of the Lord!" (Job 1:21)

As a human being designed by God to experience the rich goodness and joy of meaningful relationships, valuable possessions, satisfying accomplishments, and the realization of good dreams, the loss of each would cause deep suffering and heartache.

But this thought experiment is not intended to evaluate your response to tragedy and loss so much as it's designed to help you gauge your devotion and love. My goal is to help you ask the questions, *What is my ultimate priority?* and *In whom do I find my hope and satisfaction?* and then wrestle with your honest answers.

We give our hearts over to so many other things than God. We look to so many other things for life. I know I do. Especially the very gifts that he himself gives to us—they become more important to us than he is. That's not the way it's supposed to be. As

long as our happiness is tied to the things we can lose, we are
vulnerable.[5]

Those words from John Edredge's book, *Walking With God,* are
true. Everything you listed above can be lost. And the only way to
live a life in which you are not devastated by their loss is to tie your
heart to something—to some One, in this case—that you can never
lose.

You cannot lose God. And he will not lose you. Ever.

It is the Lord who goes before you. He will be with you; He will
not leave you or forsake you. Do not fear or be dismayed.
(Deuteronomy 31:8)

Why Name Our Idols?

Why name our idols at all? Why do the hard work to identify
and label what we consciously or unconsciously worship?
Wallace's speech helps us here too:

The insidious thing about these forms of worship is not that
they're evil or sinful, it's that they're unconscious. They are default
settings. They're the kind of worship you just gradually slip into,
day after day...without ever being fully aware that that's what
you're doing.[6]

Everyone serves a god, remember? So, the important question
is do you serve the God that's eternal and gives real life or gods that
are temporal and take life? And if you serve the latter, would you
want to know?

The Bible says the enemy we face is not of flesh and blood,[7]
and he is a thief hell-bent on destroying real life.[8] With subtle
cunning, he redirects our affections toward things that will ultimately perish. Things that, therefore, cannot ultimately satisfy.

God draws your devotion away from material things so he can give you spiritual life, while Satan directs your devotion *to* material things so he can steal your spiritual life. Satan is picking a fight, and he doesn't fight fair. Naming your idols is one of the ways we courageously engage in the battle.

Name Them All

In Acts 17, the Apostle Paul accepts an invitation from the philosophers of Athens to share with them the message he'd preached all over the city. The Athenians worshipped a pantheon of gods, and each had a name and statue. Among those literal idols was a statue dedicated to "an unknown god" (just in case they accidentally overlooked a deity or two).

Paul took the opportunity to introduce them to the God they didn't yet know, "the God who made the world and everything in it" who "doesn't live in man-made temples."[9] He helped them see that the representative statues in their pantheon of small-g gods led them to miss out on the one true God. He longed for them to know the real God, the God who "who gives life and breath to everything."[10]

Like the Athenians, our idols have names too. We worship gods called success, autonomy, technology, popularity, greed, sexual appeal, pleasurable encounters, intellectual prowess, political power, money, glory, reputation, and religion (to name only a few).

But unlike the publicly displayed Athenian idols, ours are under wraps, remaining unidentified—or ignored—until it's too late. Until, as David Foster Wallace commented, they eat us alive.

We must commit to naming our idols—the people, possessions, beliefs, and desires that hold more sway over us than God himself. Only when we bring them into the light will we recognize they are not God, reject them as imposters, and replace them with the One in whom we "live, and move, and exist."[11]

So *how* do we do that?

The answer is simple, but it won't be easy. Thankfully, the Spirit of the living God will help you all along the way. He wants us all to recognize, reject, repent of, and replace our idols so we can freely live the real life he longs to give.

Recognize

The first step toward finding a solution to any problem is being fully convinced—and admitting—that there *is* a problem. The same holds true for idolatry.

We must ask ourselves (and allow others to ask) the difficult questions about our underlying beliefs and our unexamined behaviors. Then we must be willing to face the truthful answers if we ever hope to eliminate our idols.

Our tendency in the midst of a busy life and a distracting culture is to remain swept up in the day-to-day without taking a closer look. And this problem isn't new. Isaiah, the Old Testament prophet, identified the same issue several thousand years ago, and he wrote about it beautifully and bluntly.

[The wood carver] uses part of the wood to make a fire. With it he warms himself and bakes his bread.

Then—yes, it's true—he takes the rest of it and makes himself a god to worship! He makes an idol and bows down in front of it! He burns part of the tree to roast his meat and to keep himself warm. He says, "Ah, that fire feels good."

Then he takes what's left and makes his god: a carved idol! He falls down in front of it, worshiping and praying to it. "Rescue me!" he says. "You are my god!"

Such stupidity and ignorance! Their eyes are closed, and they cannot see. Their minds are shut, and they cannot think. The person who made the idol never stops to reflect, "Why, it's just a block of wood! I burned half of it for heat and used it to bake my bread and roast my meat. How can the rest of it be a god? Should I bow down to worship a piece of wood?"

The poor, deluded fool feeds on ashes. He trusts something that can't help him at all. Yet he cannot bring himself to ask, "Is this idol that I'm holding in my hand a lie?" (Isaiah 44:15-20)

Few of us bow down to small, wooden figurines these days, but plenty of us bow down to our checking accounts, social reputation, career goals, or other perceived successes. These are also man-made, so we need to join the Prophet in asking, *Is the idol I hold in my hands (or my heart) a lie?*

Proverbs 14:12 hits the nail on the head: "There is a way that appears to be right, but in the end it leads to death."

Recognizing we are prone to idolatry is the first step to removing and replacing the idols we're tempted to worship. Make the effort, as uncomfortable as it may be, to clearly recognize them so you can take the next step and reject them.

Reject

The oft-repeated phrase—God is a gentleman—is true. He never forces you to love him. He gives us freedom to choose life or reject it,[12] and that choice includes two parts. The first is to choose life. The second is to reject death.

It's one thing to admire and desire God and commit to any and everything that is of him. It's another thing to despise and resist Satan and intentionally reject doing anything that is not of God. When it comes to rejecting our idols, submission to God and resisting Satan go hand in hand.

James wrote it this way: "Submit yourselves, then, to God. Resist the devil, and he will flee from you."[13]

The *shema*—a passage from Deuteronomy that observant Jews have recited for the last three thousand years—helps us submit and resist.

First, the submission part.

> Listen, O Israel! The Lord is our God, the Lord alone. And you must love the Lord your God with all your heart, all your soul, and all your strength. And you must commit yourselves whole-heartedly to these commands that I am giving you today. (Deuteronomy 6:4-6)

Now the resistance part.

> You must not worship any of the gods of neighboring nations. (Deuteronomy 6:15)

God's call is two fold: Embrace and commit to him and his way with all your might, *and* refuse to give any of your devotion to anyone or anything else. Submission and resistance together help us begin to win the battle against idolatry.

First, we recognize our idols, second, we reject them, and third, we repent of them.

Repent

Repentance, unfortunately, is often confused with confession. But while confession is the admission of guilt, repentance is the commitment to turnaround and walk away from that which made you guilty. Confession is the recognition of our sinfulness; repentance is the pursuit of holiness.

If pride and reputation are your idols, then repentance is the rejection of your self-righteousness and the manipulation of others' opinions about you, *and* the humble pursuit of truth and vulnerability that comes through real, deep relationships.

If you struggle with greed and materialism, then repentance is the rejection of accumulating that which you do not need *and* generously giving of that which you have.

If viewing pornography and/or engaging in sexual activity outside of marriage is sin you struggle with, then repentance is the rejection of any non-marital sexual behavior *and* the pursuit of a loving and mutual sexual relationship with only your spouse. If you are unmarried, it's abstinence from sexual activity until you are.

It's vital to remember that true repentance and the development of holiness are destined for failure if fueled only by willpower. Thankfully, the recognition, rejection, and repentance of our idols is made possible by the Holy Spirit when we replace all other pseudo-gods with God alone.

Replace

If this point is not already abundantly clear, let me make it so: Human beings like you and me can't choose *if* we worship. We can only choose *what* or *whom* we worship.

The cure to idol-worship, then, is God-worship. The only lasting way to recognize, reject, and repent of worshipping false gods is to replace them with the one true God. "Listen O Israel! The Lord is our God, the Lord alone."[14]

This truth frees us. But we are patterned beings, and our rituals —particularly those that are destructive—take time, patience, and practice to reverse. It's far easier to demolish a house than build one.

Total repentance and trust is the step-by-step process of giving God access to every unopened room of your internal life. It's allowing him to step inside, take a good look around, and clean the dust off what's good and discard what's not.

This process is long because it's painful. But God is patient, kind, and good.

The secret rooms of our heart prefer to remain undetected and uncleaned. But when you hand him the keys to each room, he does his slow but life-giving work.

I remember when God knocked on the door of a room in my heart a few years back. His gentle knock rattled the sign above the door that read "Hero".

It was—and still often is—a room in which I store the untrue and unhelpful belief that I alone can serve and save my family. I too often mistake my role as spiritual leader, servant, husband, lover, and father as one of savior. But my wife and children have a Savior, and he's not me. (Thank God for all of us!)

It's taken months and months of continual surrender to allow God to clean out that room. On my worst days I still deny the room exists. On slightly better days, I sit in front of the door like an obstinate child making sure God knows I'm not happy he's found it.

But on my very best days, I open the door for him and accompany him inside while he lovingly—without any condemnation—points out how he can transform this room by filling it with his light as the one true Savior. Letting him clean it has proven good, right, and liberating.

This is the difficult yet necessary process of idol replacement, and it's in those difficult heart cleanings that we finally allow God to sit where he should: on the throne of our lives, in the absolute highest place of honor, prestige, and value.

What Happens if You Don't Name Your Idols?

It's been said that ignorance is bliss, and I understand the temptation to ignore the darkest and most depressing things in an attempt to remain light, bright, and happy. So much in this world causes pain and many of us—including me—would rather ignore it all and just go fishing. Or binge on Netflix. Or play basketball. Or read Harry Potter. Or do whatever it is you do.

But the reality is, ignorance is *not* true bliss. And bliss is not the point. True joy, which is much deeper and lasting than "bliss" anyway, is found when we face and deal with reality.

If you don't name your idols, you'll end up like the man who refuses to acknowledge his drinking problem or the woman refusing to face her jealousy and resentment. You'll constantly run from something that will, in time, prove faster than you.

Eventually the demon catches up, and because you're so tired from running, you'll give in and let it take you over. And a life run by temporal, ungodly things is no life at all.

You were designed to give your life to something. Better put, you are designed to give your life to some *One*. When that someone is not God, it takes life without giving it back. It may provide pleasure, pride, opportunity, or temporary happiness, but it doesn't provide *real life*. Only God provides that.

What Happens if You Do Name Your Idols?

Here's the beauty of being beings built to worship: When you give your life to the real God, he gives real life back. The Bible tells us that our full life is found in Jesus[15] when we release everything to him.[16] It's in the letting go of control that we experience true purpose, meaning, hope, and joy.

Naming your idols—being specific about the people, experiences, emotions, and dreams that most capture your attention, affection, hopes, and plans—brings them into the light. And once you see them, you can name them. And as soon as you name the idol that's chasing you, it slows the chase.

Try this and see. Fight for space this week (or right now, if you can), ask God to help you name your idols, listen for Jesus to answer, then write his answers down. As soon as you drag those idols into the light, they begin to lose their power.

Recognize, reject, repent, and replace those idols, and you will achieve victory over them. They will rear their ugly heads again from time to time, and you might lose some battles to them, but the ploys of the devil need not prevent you from living your real life in God. Satan was defeated at the cross of Calvary. The war is not yet over, but it is won.

How I Practice Rule #10

When it comes to naming my idols, there are two practices I find very helpful. The first is an ancient prayer practice that helps me eliminate distractions and slow my mind and heart long enough to actually identify my idols.

The second practice is a difficult but crucial one. I confide in a close, faithful friend, telling him the truth about what I idolize. Here's how I engage both practices.

The prayer practice is called Daily Examen, and it was developed by the founder of the Jesuits, Ignatius of Loyola. Ignatius believed the Bible's teaching that Jesus is with us by his Spirit all day, every day. The Daily Examen helps you reflect on the events of your day to detect God's presence and discern his direction. When practiced over time, it's a very helpful tool for naming your idols. Here's how it works.

Set aside twenty minutes at the end of your day to do the following:

1. *Become aware of God's presence.*

Settle in to a quiet space, breathe deeply, and set your mind on God and his presence with you.

2. *Review the day with gratitude.*

Take a mental walk through the events of the day, expressing gratitude to God for life and all that he's given.

3. *Pay attention to your emotions.*

As you recall the events and conversations of the day, make note of how they make you feel.

4. Choose one feature of the day and pray from it.

Identify a moment, conversation, person, or event and the emotions around it. Use it to ignite your conversation with God. Talk honestly with him about it.

5. Look forward to tomorrow.

Take a mental peek at the day ahead, asking God to help you recognize his presence in each moment of the next twenty-four hours.[17]

How does this simple process help you name your idols? As you review your day, you will become aware of how, where, and to whom your energy and focus are given.

Do you notice a habit that pops up every single day? That might be an idol that needs to be named.

Do you notice that the most emotional—high or low—points in your day center on food, alcohol, entertainment, or a particular person? Perhaps there's an idol there that needs to be identified.

Do you notice that you are altogether unaware of God during the hours of nine to five, or when you are at your computer, or on your phone, or traveling for work? The pattern could be signaling an idol.

Last thing: the Daily Examen is not about guilt. God loves you and is pleased with you because of his Son, Jesus. You do not need to perform for him or prove your worth to him. You are valuable to him because he created you, died for you, and because he says so.[18] So don't let the enemy of God turn this helpful practice into a tool to beat you down.

Rather, let it become a practice that connects you with your God and King, and allow him to bring you into deeper, better, and fuller life.

The second practice is by far the most difficult, but it's also the most freeing. It's the practice of confession.

The book of James includes this encouragement:

Confess your sins to each other and pray for each other so that
you may be healed. The earnest prayer of a righteous person has
great power and produces wonderful results. (James 5:16)

The point of confession is to drag that which kills us into the
Light that saves us. And the practice is simple. It's not *easy*, but it's
simple. Here's how to do it.

1. *Ask for a friend.* - Spiritual friendship is something God
   made for us and made us for (see Rule #5, Join the
   Church). Ask him to help you identify a faithful friend
   with whom you can partner to name your idols.
2. *Agree with your friend.* - Talk openly and honestly with
   each other about God's Word and idolatry. Once you're
   on the same page about what idolatry is and why it's
   crucial to name it, the two of you are ready to fight—
   and win—together.
3. *Fight with your friend.* - Now that you agree with God
   and each other about the nature of idolatry, it's time to
   share one of your idols. This won't be easy, but if *you*
   share with integrity and vulnerability, your friend will
   too, and you'll both begin to see how idols lose their
   power when we are brave enough to name them.
4. *Pray with your friend.* - Last but not least, pray together.
   Thank God for friendship and lean into God's
   forgiveness and freedom. Assure one another that
   although the battle isn't over, it is won. And don't forget
   to celebrate the victories when they come.

May God bless you as you do the difficult thing, and may these
words from 1 John be your theme as you trust him, trust others, and
name your idols.

If we walk in the light, as he is in the light, we have fellowship
with one another, and the blood of Jesus his Son cleanses us from
all sin. (1 John 1:7 ESV)

———

I pray that you are a Christian who is keenly aware that there's no
hope, life, or salvation in anyone or anything other than God the
Father, Son, and Holy Spirit.[19] I pray that you know what many
other worshippers of God know: When we live with Jesus as the
undisputed champion of our lives we live in unparalleled vitality.

But, like you, I too get distracted and derailed. The world
disagrees with our proclamation that Jesus is Lord and that God is
the unequivocal center of life, the only real deity. The contrary
messages bombard us at every turn as Satan fights furiously to
siphon our devotion away from God.

But when the other "gods" come calling, you can trust the real
one and ask for his help to recognize, reject, repent of, and replace
every idol. Remember, God "is a strong fortress; the godly run to
him and are safe,"[20] and he will never leave us or forsake us.[21]

Those two truths—that God is our strength, and he is ever-
present—are never more needed or proven true than in the midst
of suffering. And a book about real life with God must address the
problem of pain. So, we turn now to the most counterintuitive, and
perhaps most underappreciated, of all the 12 Rules: Embrace Your
Suffering.

11

EMBRACE YOUR SUFFERING

"Perhaps in the breaking of precious things, something even more precious than we can imagine might be unleashed."
—Jay Wolf

There's one common human denominator: suffering. There's not a person on the planet who has not, does not, or will not suffer.

And we hate it. We despise suffering. And rightfully so. Suffering is one of the great tragedies of human life. But our hatred for what's wrong about pain causes us to create an idol out of what's right about painlessness.

Many of us worship comfort.

It's easy to misdiagnose our modern obsession with possessions as materialism and our compulsive device-use as technology addiction. But for many, the true culprit is bigger: It's comfort idolatry.

The technologically advanced West offers the perfect case study of this. We have air-conditioned homes, safe and efficient vehicles, affordable airline travel, ubiquitous internet connection, and more food in one grocery store that an entire village in West Africa.

Yet we can't seem to stamp out suffering. No matter when, where, and how we try to control it, it rears its ugly head in new ways.

The reason for this is twofold. First, as a rapidly secularizing culture, we've forgotten that the reason for suffering is sin. Which means we've forgotten that the cure is a savior.

In our unconscious forgetfulness—or our knowing denial—we've stopped looking for a redeemer. Instead we put our hope in medical technology, sociological solutions, and political progress, losing sight altogether that sin infiltrated each of those disciplines eons ago.

The second reason for our struggle with suffering is that we are afraid or unwilling to embrace it. We are so deeply convinced that pain ought to be eradicated—or somehow escaped or anesthetized—that the very proposition that hardship and heartache might have positive value is cultural blasphemy.

But what if your pain, your difficulty, your hardship was *good* for you? What if, given the existence of suffering because of sin, God not only promises one day to save us from it but also promises to make it useful in the meantime?

What if (and I know these are BIG what-ifs), the promise that "God works for the good of those who love him, who have been called according to his purpose"[1] *includes* suffering?

What if the key for you to endure your suffering in our sin-filled world was not eliminating it but *embracing* it?

The Pain Is Worth the Cure

Jesus was not afraid to suffer when it was purpose-filled. In fact, the Bible tells us in Hebrews 12 that "Because of the joy awaiting him, he endured the cross, disregarding its shame."[2]

Jesus endured untold and unparalleled spiritual, physical, and emotional trauma by bearing our sin on Calvary's cross. Excruciating is too light a word for his suffering.

Yet, the Bible tells us he endured the shame of all humanity's sin on that cross "because of the joy awaiting him." In other words, there was a purpose, a reason, a deeply desired outcome that could be achieved only through Jesus' sacrifice.

His suffering was anything but useless or gratuitous. It was purpose-driven, powerful, and it accomplished something grand.

The way Jesus talked about and dealt with suffering is instructive for us. He both cured it *and* endured it when it proved an opportunity for the glory of God and the good of people. Here is what I mean.

In John chapters 9 and 11, the apostle recounts when Jesus told his listeners that an individual's suffering is not about them at all. It serves a much greater divine purpose.

In John 9 Jesus and his disciples came upon a man who was born blind. The disciples asked him, "Why was this man born blind? Was it because of his own sins or his parents' sins?"[3]

Their question reveals their personal and cultural ideas regarding suffering. This man, they figured, was blind because of a specific sin in his life or in his parents' life. They did not consider a third option. So Jesus gave it to them.

"It was not because of his sins or his parents' sins," Jesus answered. "This happened so the power of God could be seen in him."[4]

And when Jesus healed him by that power the entire town was captivated. They wondered aloud to the man, "Who healed you?"[5] and "How did he do it?"[6] and "Where is he now?"[7]

The man's suffering—and Jesus' healing of it—served to show God's might and reign. It showed that his kingdom had truly come in Jesus.

Two chapters later, John tells the story of Jesus' dear friend, Lazarus. Lazarus grew sick, and his sisters sent a message to Jesus regarding his imminent death and asking that Jesus come and heal him.

Pay close attention to Jesus' response. He said, "Lazarus' sickness will not end in death. No, it happened for the glory of God so that the Son of God will receive glory from this."[8]

Jesus' friends and disciples must have been mighty confused when Lazarus died. Didn't Jesus just say that Lazarus's sickness would *not* end in death?

A few days passed before Jesus finally hit the road to visit Lazarus's tomb and grieving family. But once he did, he made this bold statement: "Lazarus is dead. And for your sakes, I'm glad I wasn't there, for now you will really believe."[9]

Convinced of the benefits of this momentary suffering, Jesus let death linger. He did not hurry. He did not seek to solve the problem or ease the pain until the Father's timing was right. But when that time came, he performed the most mouth-dropping miracle of them all.

Jesus walked up to Lazarus's grave and reminded the onlookers, "Didn't I tell you that you would see God's glory if you believe?"[10] Then he shouted, "Lazarus, come out!"[11]

And you know what? *The dead man walked.*

Lazarus came out of the tomb as alive as he was before he went in.

Jesus never dismisses the sadness that suffering brings,[12] but he also never skips past the opportunity pain provides. Jesus knows the beauty of the outcome outweighs the pain of the process.

This truth is never more apparent than in Jesus' own death and resurrection experience.

The Great Embrace

All the wonder working of Jesus' three-year ministry culminated in a final horrific scene. Jesus, the Lamb of God who came to take away the sin of the world, was led to slaughter.

In the final moments before his showdown with death, Jesus revisited the Garden of Gethsemane where he humbly embraced his suffering. Matthew, Mark, and Luke all recorded the prayer Jesus prayed that night and the sheer agony of the moment.

After sharing a meal, Jesus and his loyal companions made the short hike to the Garden of Gethsemane. There, in light of pending doom, Jesus asked them all to pray with him.

He confided in his closest friends—Peter, James, and John. "My soul is crushed with grief to the point of death." Then he asked them, "Stay here and keep watch with me."[13]

Jesus went on a little farther to speak with the Father alone. There he prayed the crucial prayer.

> My Father! If it is possible, let this cup of suffering be taken away from me. Yet I want your will to be done, not mine. (Matthew 26:39)

Luke's Gospel tells us Jesus was in such agony, praying with such fervency, that "his sweat became like great drops of blood falling down to the ground."[14]

When it comes to Jesus' embrace of his suffering, it's vital we recognize his humanity.

Did Jesus *want* to suffer? By no means! He was God in the flesh, not a masochist. Jesus the man cried out to God the Father for another way. But he was also unyielding in his submission, and he embraced the very real possibility that this was the best way.

It's here that some close Bible study is very helpful. If you examine each of Jesus' prayers in Matthew's account, you can see the progression of his conversation with God.

Verse thirty-nine tells us that Jesus desired to do God's will but boldly asked for this "cup of suffering" to be taken away.

Then in verse forty-two, Jesus' second prayer began with an acknowledgment, not a plea. He prayed, "If this cup cannot be taken away unless I drink it, your will be done."[15]

Jesus heard from the Father after his first prayer. God said that the cup must indeed be taken by Jesus.

Finally, Matthew tells us in verse forty-four that Jesus "went to pray a third time, saying the same things again."[16] After final confirmation, Jesus took hold of his destiny, saying to his companions, "The time has come... Up, let's be going. Look, my betrayer is here!"[17]

By the time Judas Iscariot led the soldiers into Jesus' garden, Jesus had met with the Father and embraced the suffering that must come.

Now that we've done a little Bible study, let's do some theological work.

The temptation here is to still focus on the cure. After all, God raised Jesus to brand new life only a few days after the horrifying crucifixion. That's true. But *here* is what's important: The saving work of God occurred while Jesus died on Friday's cross, not when he strolled out of Sunday's tomb.

You see, the resurrection is the promise of new life, while the cross is the power over sin's curse. It's so counterintuitive, isn't it? What we see in the resurrection is a picture of our future. A future life beyond the grave in which we are made whole, the way it was intended to be from the beginning.

But what we are given on the cross through Jesus the suffering servant is the actual *defeat* of sin and death itself! It's in God's *suffering* that we are redeemed.

As the prophet Isaiah told us,

> But he was pierced for our transgressions, he was crushed for our iniquities; the punishment that brought us peace was on him, and by his wounds we are healed. We all, like sheep, have gone astray, each of us has turned to our own way; and the Lord has laid on him the iniquity of us all. (Isaiah 53:5-6)

Jesus embraced his suffering, and God saved us all through it.

And believe it or not, God can—and does—do miraculous things in and through *our* suffering today. When we embrace him as we embrace it, he redeems our pain.

Embracing God

Embracing our suffering really means to embrace *God* in our suffering.

God is not just a pain fixer. He's more than a Band-Aid, a pill, a surgeon, a miracle worker. He is the One who makes us whole, who completes us. He redeems us and all suffering, and he is our ultimate and only home.

If that's all true, then we are able to reach out to him, find hope in him, and rest in him even when we suffer. *Particularly* when we suffer.

As we grab hold of him, releasing ourselves to allow him to grab hold of us, we can accept our suffering as an opportunity to sink into his embrace and participate in his redemption of our darkest moments.

Christians lean on the belief that God will transform human existence into the joy-filled, mutually beneficial and cooperative, perfectly whole and fulfilling experience it's supposed to be. We trust Scripture when it tells us that the summation of all things is in God himself[18] and that future reality is terrific in its beauty, goodness, rightness, and perfection.[19]

But if you're like me, you sometimes forget that God's redemption is not just a future cosmic reality. In his presence, by his power and for his purposes, God rescues us and redeems our experiences *now*. And when we look through the pain, embrace the opportunities in it, and hold fast in the presence of God, we find that the most beautiful of flowers bloom in the dark.

Active Embrace

But what does it look like to embrace our suffering? How do we do it? And what—exactly—does it produce?

As a human being who suffers like you, I'm convinced by God's Word and experience that embracing our suffering produces maturity, freedom, mission opportunities, experiences with God, worship, clarity about reality, and best of all, a deepened relationship with the good God of the universe.

Let's look at each and see if suffering really can be this good.

Suffering: A Vehicle to Maturity

The apostles Paul and James wrote words that shock the contemporary mind. In fact, I venture to say that if you've read the following verses while suffering, they likely frustrated—or infuriated—you. But we must take a look.

Paul wrote the following:

We can rejoice, too, when we run into problems and trials, for we know that they help us develop endurance. And endurance develops strength of character, and character strengthens our confident hope of salvation. (Romans 5:3-4)

James echoed this teaching when he wrote this:

Dear brothers and sisters, when troubles of any kind come your way, consider it an opportunity for great joy. For you know that when your faith is tested, your endurance has a chance to grow. So let it grow, for when your endurance is fully developed, you will be perfect and complete, needing nothing. (James 1:2-4)

How could these men—both of whom suffered greatly—tell

others to "rejoice" during hardship and consider suffering an opportunity for "great joy"? Were they crazy?

Upon further review, it doesn't seem that Paul and James were insane. Rather, they maintained a keen understanding of the goal and prioritized it above their current circumstances.

Paul told sufferers to rejoice in trials *because* God develops something eternally valuable through them. Similarly, James had joy even in dire circumstances *because* those difficult situations afforded opportunities for growth. And it's not just any kind of growth; it's growth in Jesus that makes Christians "perfect and complete, needing nothing."

Let's be clear: Neither man celebrated pain. They longed for what it *produced*. Both men suffered with the end in mind. They so deeply valued spiritual growth and maturity that no matter how ugly and difficult the process, their joy was never displaced.

Jesus too looked beyond the pain. He focused on God's outcome and endured the greatest of all suffering.[20] He knew something we must all remember: the joy, endurance, character, hope, and relationship with God that are achieved through the passageway of pain are worth it.

Spiritual maturity is not gained by escaping our suffering. We mature into our best selves by resting in the power, presence, and promises of God *as* we suffer.

Suffering: Prison or Freedom?

Suffering carries with it the possibility to release us rather than imprison us. If we allow him, God will use suffering to set us free from our devotion to perishable things so we can cling to him alone.

The Bible never shies away from the reality of suffering. Scholars believe Job is the earliest written book in the Bible, and its central theme is human suffering.

The central figure, and the book's namesake, was Job—a man

among boys on Earth. In God's words, Job was "blameless and upright, a man who fears God and shuns evil,"[21] and he was blessed with a huge family and had amassed massive wealth.

God allowed the devil to take everything from Job, including his wealth, family, and health. Yet in the middle of his exquisite suffering, Job fell to the ground and worshipped. He proclaimed, "The Lord gave and the Lord has taken away; may the name of the Lord be praised."[22]

The epic suffering he endured revealed his priorities: He was God's man, more concerned about worship and relationship with God than his own comfort and welfare.

The rest of the story reveals cracks in Job's armor, similar to ours. He was not perfect, but God was right about him. Job was a man of deep faith and trust, and his suffering—no matter how intense—did not become his prison.

The rich young man we discussed in Rule #8 offers a much different view. The very idea of reducing his considerable wealth drove him away from God, not toward him.[23] He wasn't free, like Job. He was imprisoned by his wealth and comfort. Ironically, suffering the loss of his possessions, wealth, and social standing, would have freed him if he had embraced it.

In his second letter to the Corinthian church, Paul wrote:

> We think you ought to know, dear brothers and sisters, about the trouble we went through in the province of Asia. We were crushed and overwhelmed beyond our ability to endure, and we thought we would never live through it. In fact, we expected to die.
>
> But as a result, we stopped relying on ourselves and learned to rely only on God, who raises the dead. And he did rescue us from mortal danger, and he will rescue us again. We have placed our confidence in him, and he will continue to rescue us. (2 Corinthians 1:8-10)

The truth is that we *say* we rely on God. And we may even believe it. Suffering often proves whether that's true or false.

By God's great goodness, suffering reveals our true level of dependence, and increases it. Suffering can be the gift we always needed to develop in us the reliance on God we cannot live without.

Suffering: From Misery to Mission

When the COVID-19 pandemic and subsequent government lockdown gripped the world in early 2020, our congregation's pastors and elders decided to focus everyone's attention on the book of Philippians. We weren't the only church to do so.

Many were drawn to this short book because Paul wrote it during his own lockdown. He was under arrest for crimes he didn't commit, and this letter helps all of us develop a missional perspective on our suffering. In Paul's words,

> Now I want you to know, brothers and sisters, that what has happened to me has actually served to advance the gospel. As a result, it has become clear throughout the whole palace guard and to everyone else that I am in chains for Christ. And because of my chains, most of the brothers and sisters have become confident in the Lord and dare all the more to proclaim the gospel without fear. (Philippians 1:12-14)

Paul was so devoted to God and so transformed by the good news about Jesus, that he thanked and worshiped God for his suffering and hardship because it afforded opportunities to share that good news in new ways, to new people, through new circumstances.

Suffering is a terrible result of sin in a fallen world. We are right to want it to end. But when submitted to Jesus, it can become a part of our ministry. "What has happened to me has actually served to advance the gospel," Paul wrote.

Suffering sometimes puts you in unique places or relationships providing opportunities to bear witness to Jesus with folks you would not otherwise meet.

Paul's house arrest included twenty-four-hour surveillance by a Roman soldier. The guards believed they held Paul captive, but Paul believed God held *them* captive. God provided the audience, Paul preached the sermons.

This perspective transforms suffering from a self-centered problem to a gospel-centered pulpit.

The second way in which God turns misery into mission is through your hard-earned empathy. Again, Paul's words are eye-opening and invigorating:

> All praise to God, the Father of our Lord Jesus Christ. God is our merciful Father and the source of all comfort. He comforts us in all our troubles so that we can comfort others. When they are troubled, we will be able to give them the same comfort God has given us. (2 Corinthians 1:3-4)

Our hardship and heartache provide opportunities to enter into another's pain with them. More than pity, our own experiences of suffering allow us to empathize. Others can draw God's comfort, practical guidance, and spiritual hope from our relatable experience.

This reality transforms our tragedy from useless to useful, and it imbues our pain with purpose. By God's grace we can move from wallowing in misery to living on mission.

Suffering: A Taste of Divinity

Have you ever pondered what it is like to be God? All of us attempt to assume the throne from time to time, but have you really considered what it's like to be him—to experience what he experiences, to see what he sees, to feel what he feels? Suffering, believe it or not, offers one such peek into the life of the Divine.

I once heard a woman in the midst of deep suffering say, "If my severe and chronic pain allows me to experience an ounce of the pain Jesus endured on my behalf, then I am grateful for it."

This is a mind-shifting, life-changing, suffering-redeeming mentality. And it opens a number of other joy-inducing ways we can relate to God.

When we create, we're like our Creator.

When we forgive, we walk in the footsteps of the Father.

When we live in loving community, we taste the Trinity.

We will never be God, but suffering—as painful as it is—provides an opportunity to relate experientially to the God who endured the greatest trial on our behalf. God became like us. He experienced what we experience. He injected himself into humanity—as a *human*—and walked where mere mortals trod.

In Hebrews chapter four, the Bible reminds us of this reality.

> Since we have a great High Priest who has entered heaven, Jesus the Son of God, let us hold firmly to what we believe. This High Priest of ours understands our weaknesses, for he faced all of the same testings we do, yet he did not sin. (Hebrews 4:14-15)

Jesus is far more than a sympathizer. He walked our walk, felt our pain, lived our life.

Remember when Jesus shed tears of sorrow and anger at Lazarus's tomb?[24] Remember when he was tempted by Satan to cheat on God in the desert?[25] Remember the time when he longed for and asked for a less painful way in the Garden of Gethsemane? [26] Jesus knows what it's like to be *you*.

But let's flip the script. Suffering is an opportunity for us to know what it's like to be him.

It may only scratch the surface because he is so incomprehensible, so different, so wholly *not* human, but because he became human, our experience enmeshes with his. And that's a gift. Even if that gift is presented in pain.

If you and I embrace our pain, we can connect with the God of the universe in a specific and surreal way. He knows us better through his suffering, and we know him better through ours. This perspective is rare, but it's also rich and rewarding.

Suffering: A Reality Check

There's an ancient Hebrew word you may have heard: *shalom*. It's most often translated as "peace," but pastor and theologian Cornelius Plantinga provides a much fuller definition.

> The webbing together of God, humans, and all creation in justice, fulfillment, and delight is what the Hebrew prophets call *shalom*. We call it peace, but it means far more... In the Bible, shalom means *universal flourishing, wholeness, and delight*—a rich state of affairs in which natural needs are satisfied and natural gifts are fruitfully employed, a state of affairs that inspires joyful wonder as its Creator and Savior opens doors and welcomes the creatures in whom he delights. *Shalom*, in other words, is the way things ought to be.[27]

This beautiful, mutual, and selfless way of living is how God intended it, and praise be to God, it's the way it will be again.[28] But for now, the ubiquity of pain and hardship is a visceral reminder that things are *not* the way they ought to be.

But if we remain dialed in to God's good promises, our pain can raise a flag of hope and become a reminder that help is coming. The very existence of our suffering sounds the alarm, telling us all is not well and we need God, and it stirs our desire for his rescue and restoration.

Even if the only thing your suffering does is remind you that the world is broken and we can't fix it, let it do that work. Let it remind you that humans are insufficient. We need God.

Humans have tried everything. Many of our efforts solve many a problem, but none solve *the* problem. None of them bring *shalom.*

And so we wait. We wait on the One who can and will do what we are unable to do. And our suffering, if nothing else, points us to him and our glorious suffering-free future together.

Suffering: Kindling for Relationship

Two of the men in the Old Testament whom I admire are King Jehoshaphat and Nehemiah.

In 2 Chronicles 20, King Jehoshaphat received troubling news. His enemies amassed an army and were headed his direction. By the time Jehoshaphat received the news, they were already on his doorstep.

Here's how he responded: "Alarmed, Jehoshaphat resolved to inquire of the Lord, and he proclaimed a fast for all Judah."[29]

Nehemiah, the Jewish exile who served the king of Babylon in fifth century B.C., also received bad news. A messenger told Nehemiah, "Those who survived the exile and are back in the province are in great trouble and disgrace."[30] The people of his homeland were in dire straits.

How did he respond to the news that worried his soul? He "sat down and wept." Then "for some days [Nehemiah] mourned and fasted and prayed before the God of heaven."[31]

Do you see why I admire these men? When suffering threatened, they stepped into God's presence through prayer. When my boat is rocked, I hope to follow their lead.

For these men, among many others we see in the Scriptures and in life, hardship produced an opportunity for prayer. Suffering became a catalyst for intimacy, a kindling for relationship.

Yes, of course these men prayed for practical solutions to the pressing problem. And God answered, provided, and protected in remarkable ways (check out God's answer to Jehoshaphat in 2 Chronicles 20 and to Nehemiah in Nehemiah 1-2).

But what I see in these men's lives is more than just a request for a bailout. Their trials presented the chance to step into the very presence of their God and lead others to do the same.

What if you and I viewed our seasons of suffering as occasions to deepen our relationship with God, not just get something from him? I daresay if I viewed suffering this way, I would be more willing and able to embrace it.

Nobody escapes the suffering sin produces. But here's a radical question: Instead of dreading those moments, why not anticipate the depth they can bring to your relationship with God? Why not surrender now to the idea that locked up inside our pain-inducing circumstances is an opportunity to develop our connection with the Creator?

If you and I are serious about authentic prayer and deepened relationship, if we are serious about growing our desire for and dependence on God, and if we are serious about knowing how God speaks and the kind of comfort his presence provides, would we not have a different perspective on life's pain-filled moments?

If we are wise, we will recognize that pain can serve as far more than just the spark for sporadic outbursts to God. Rather, it can be the impetus for authentic conversation and real relationship.

And if God is God, and prayer is a lifeline to him, then isn't it a gift when anything, including suffering, causes us to reach out for him? I'm one sufferer who thinks it is.

Embrace: Not Seek, Permit, or Cause

With all of the above in mind, I must offer a clarification. As already acknowledged, we cannot escape suffering. But you also must not seek to suffer, cause others to suffer, or permit suffering if you are able to stop it. That is sinful, and it is *not* what I'm advocating.

Embrace Your Suffering is a spiritual posture with physical and practical steps. It's holding fast to God himself, maintaining hope for the renewal of all things, and enduring what's broken and scarred. It's also purposefully seeking *shalom* by aiding those who suffer, eliminating suffering wherever we can, and never intentionally contributing to it.

Embracing your suffering is Jehoshaphat praying *and* going to battle.

It's Nehemiah praying *and* leading the effort to rebuild his city.

It's Jesus praying "My Father! If it is possible, let this cup of suffering be taken away from me"[32] *and* going to the cross for the Father's glory and our good.

Embracing our suffering allows for the biblical inevitability that all things will be redeemed by God and made to work for his glory, others' good, and our joy.[33] Both today and for eternity.

It's believing that we can joyfully endure because endurance "develops strength of character, and character strengthens our confident hope of salvation."[34]

It means that we trust that when God works in our lives, including our pain, we become "fully developed... perfect and complete, needing nothing."[35]

What Happens if You Don't Embrace Your Suffering?

One thing in particular results from failing to think faithfully about suffering and embracing it as an opportunity. That one thing is crippling resentment.

The unbelieving world tends to blame God for what's wrong with the world. Ironically, many in the church's ranks do the same thing. But if God is the source of suffering, then you are a victim of God's negligence (at best) or his malicious intent (at worst). That god is not worthy of worship.

But, if your theology on sin and suffering is sound, it enables you to put the problem where the problem lies: on free human beings' rebellion against God. Then, and only then, can you cling to the God who is so good that he rescues and redeems us from the bed *we* made.

Now we must be careful here. I am not saying that you, as an individual, are the cause of all your suffering. Other humans may have caused you great harm, and that's not your fault. It's their fault. That must be said, and it must be said clearly.

But, thinking more broadly, we realize sin's plague broke the world and infects us all. If you are unclear about humanity's ultimate role in the existence and continuation of sin, you will forever resent God, believing he is at fault.

And when you begin to resent God every time you suffer, you heap more suffering upon yourself. Your inability to separate yourself emotionally from your circumstances will imprison you.

Some of you may not know what I'm talking about. Perhaps you enjoyed an emotionally healthy upbringing. Maybe you've always had mature, faithful relationships. If so, that's wonderful, and you can praise and thank God for his grace in your life.

But some of you know *exactly* what I'm talking about. You've lived it. Repeatedly. Your life is one full of abuse and hardship, trial and pain. You, of all my readers, are struggling the most with this chapter.

But you, my dear friend, are also the one who can gain the most from embracing your suffering.

What Happens if You Do Embrace Your Suffering?

If you embrace your suffering, you will experience freedom from it. That's how powerful God's truth about this is.

You may not experience relief from it, but you will experience freedom from it. And relief and freedom are not the same thing.

Relief is a break from the symptoms, the pain, and the situation that causes your suffering. Freedom from suffering is much deeper and better. Freedom from suffering means you are not controlled by your painful circumstances, and it opens you to hope and redemption, *even* if the pain is never assuaged.

Embracing your suffering allows you to move beyond it, even if not out of it. It creates opportunities to unite with the God who suffered and to watch as he redeems your pain in ways you did not previously imagine.

A life without purpose is a painful loss. A life with purpose is focused, fruitful, and free. So it is with pain. Pain without purpose is caustic, corrosive, and captures us. Pain with purpose grows us, matures us, and binds us to the One who is our ultimate freedom.

How I Practice Rule #11

Sometimes the most counterintuitive action produces the best results.

My first car was a 1985 Nissan pickup. For those of you who have ever driven a vehicle that old, you know there's no such thing as "bells and whistles."

It's an engine. Inside a body. On four tires. And that's about it.

My old truck didn't have anti-lock brakes, so my dad shared an important tip with me. Should I start to skid on a rainy day, he said, I should stay calm and "pump the brakes." Instead of pushing the brake pedal further to the floor, he instructed me to lift my foot *off* the brake before applying it again.

Do you have any idea how difficult that is? When your tires slide on slick pavement the most difficult thing to do is take your foot *off* the brake. Everything in you wants to jam it through the floorboard.

Several winters later, I drove through town as some of the rain turned into sleet. As I put on the brakes for a red light, my little blue truck started to skid. If I didn't act fast, I was headed into the intersection. Dad's words flashed through my mind: "Pump the brakes."

Somehow, I overrode my natural impulse and yanked my foot

from the brake. It was terrifying. Quickly but gently, I applied it again. Off, then on. Off, then on. Pumping the brakes.

And sure enough, each time I took my foot off the break I could feel the tires engage the road more solidly. In the end, I came to a stop well ahead of the intersection. And a whole new reality came true for me.

Similar to pumping the brakes, praising God can be a counter-intuitive but life-saving action. When you're sliding through suffer-ing, one of the most difficult things to do is to lift yourself off the floor and praise God. But when you do, you will feel the tires of your life engage the road again. Your heart and mind find traction in the truth of God's goodness, power, work, and redemption, despite the moment's terrible circumstances.

For this very purpose God provided the Psalms, a dynamic list of praise lyrics for our darkest hours. These ancient poems and songs cover the full gamut of human experience. Their authors never shy away from life's pain and confusion, and yet they always steer us back to God's faithfulness and presence.

The practice for this Rule is simple: Praise God by praying the Psalms.

When hardship hits, embrace God by pulling out your Bible and reading the Psalms aloud. You can start at Psalm 1 and read one every day or return again and again to one of your favorites. Let the psalmists' laments lead yours. Adopt their praises as your own.

When you are able to do nothing else, just read. Read aloud. Read every day. And the Spirit of the living God will meet you and mend you.

In one of the darkest periods of our lives, my wife was led to Psalm 105. It was a gift from the Holy Spirit. When all was wrong with the world these words of God buoyed us in the darkness, drawing us up to—and into—Him.

Give thanks to the Lord and proclaim his greatness.

Let the whole world know what he has done.

Sing to him; yes, sing his praises.

Tell everyone about his wonderful deeds.

Exult in his holy name;

rejoice, you who worship the Lord.

Search for the Lord and for his strength;

continually seek him.

Remember the wonders he has performed,

his miracles, and the rulings he has given,

you children of his servant Abraham,

you descendants of Jacob, his chosen ones.

He is the Lord our God.

His justice is seen throughout the land.

He always stands by his covenant—

the commitment he made to a thousand generations. (Psalm 105:1-8)

Something profound and deeply spiritual happens when we turn our eyes to Heaven and declare, either in our words or his, the true goodness of God.

Praising God in the most difficult of moments rights the ship. It doesn't solve all our problems, but it places our hearts and minds back into the hands of God and allows us to see everything clearly. It provides the traction our souls need to trust, hope, and endure.

As you work hard to embrace your suffering, psalms of praise will help focus your pain-filled vision on the One who offers redemption, hope, and healing—either now or in the life to come.

———

Pain and suffering are a problem. They are the shadowy underbelly of a broken world, the sorrowful symptoms of a world drowning in sin. And all of us long for the day when God will eradicate pain and suffering forever. But one of God's greatest gifts to humanity is the way he works in us and for us when we embrace what he alone can do in and through our suffering.

Trust God and embrace your suffering—allowing him to change your perspective on what is possible in your pain—and you will mature in faith, experience freedom, engage in his mission, experience and glorify him, live in true reality, and find doors to a deeper relationship with your Redeemer.

God is so good that when we trust and allow him, he transforms our suffering. But that is only part of the good news.

The full story is news that everyone needs to hear. Which is why the twelfth and final Rule in 12 Rules for a Christian Life is Share the Gospel. As you'll discover, the gospel is a remarkable announcement that the world desperately needs you to share *and* a message your heart desperately needs you to remember.

12

SHARE THE GOSPEL

"For this is how God loved the world: he gave his one and only Son."
—Jesus

The late, great Christian philosopher and author Dallas Willard once wrote, "Grace is not opposed to effort, it is opposed to earning."[1]

Chew on that for a minute.

Willard knew something we all need to know. One of Satan's most devious ploys is to convince Christians that God's grace is earned. But the truth is, God's grace vehemently opposes earning.

God's love, your standing with him, and the world's redemption are only because of his grace. They are based on nothing you or I have done.[2] The Bible undergirds Willard's claim: God's grace is opposed to earning.

But the other part of Willard's quote is also true. Grace is not opposed to effort. Once a human being like you or me accepts and receives God's unbelievable gift of grace, there's plenty we get to do.

The effort and energy you used to spend on life outside God's family is now spent as a member of his family, and your God-given desires to live, love, and work become devoted to him and his kingdom.

But the effort you expend *for* God is not what earns your standing *with* God. For instance, none of these 12 Rules earns you a seat at God's table. Jesus alone did that. These are practices for enjoying your relationship with him, not for establishing it.

This is a terribly difficult reality for most of us to comprehend. Our secular society is a meritocracy. The very heart of our way of life says, "You get what you deserve" and "You are what you do" and it's up to you to "make a way for yourself." Our cultural paradigm declares that one's value, identity, and standing with others are earned, not given.

Thankfully, God's gift flies in the face of that paradigm. God gives extravagantly with no need for or expectation of payment. In Jesus, God provides rest from our vain efforts to earn a place in his family and frees us up to work with him out of gratitude rather than obligation.

This is why the Gospel is such good news.

What Is the Gospel?

But what, exactly, is "the Gospel"?

Bible translators translate the ancient Greek word *euangélion* into the English word "gospel." Literally, *euangélion* is a message, an announcement, a proclamation of good news. Like a front-page headline announcing the war is over or the message that the baby is here and healthy, the Gospel announces a long-awaited moment of goodness, beauty, renewal, and life.

That news—according to the Bible itself—is so good that it is, without hyperbole, the best and most important message ever proclaimed to anyone in the human race. Period.

But what's the content of the Bible's good news? And what does it mean for those who hear it?

The message's content differs slightly depending on where you read it in the Bible and who proclaims it, but all-in-all, it's one unified message about what the one true God accomplishes through his one and only Son on behalf of each of us.

The Gospel: As Preached by Jesus

The book of Mark hits the ground running. Mark skipped Jesus' birth narrative to immediately focus on his ministry, and in just thirteen verses, he describes Jesus' baptism, God's declaration of Jesus' sonship, the Holy Spirit's descent onto Jesus, and Jesus' desert showdown with Satan.

Then in verse 15, Mark recorded Jesus' first sermon. And what did he preach? The Gospel.

> "The time has come," he said. "The kingdom of God has come near. Repent and believe the good news!" (Mark 1:15)

The good news Jesus couldn't wait to proclaim was that he was here. And all of God's power, presence, reign, and glory came with him.

For some of us, the idea of a kingdom is vague. But first-century Jews understood kingdoms very well.

A kingdom is any place or territory in which the king is present —in person or in authority—and what he wants to happen, happens. Jesus' good news to the people was that the kingdom of God was now at hand. Jesus the King had come, and his will would be done.

For centuries, Jewish prophets predicted the Messiah would be a king ordained by God who would usher in God's permanent rule and reign. Many Jews longed for God to send a king who would free them from Roman occupation and reestablish them as God's promised people, the envy of nations. The devout waited on the edge of their seats for this king.

But their understanding of God's mission and Jesus' role in it turned out to be amiss. God's plan was not to bring a king *to* them so they could rule like in the old days. His plan was to provide the one true King *through* them who would rule in a completely new way.

Instead of sending a human king, God *himself* was now among them. The kingdom he planned, he also inaugurated, and if his people would turn from their old ways and trust this good news message, they would experience life as it was meant to be experienced.

Those who encountered and followed Jesus heard the news and tasted its amazing fruit. The blind saw. The spiritually captive were freed. The poor heard and received the good news. And God's favor was explicit in Jesus' speech, touch, and way.[3]

In one of my favorite old movies, *Tombstone*, the lead character, Wyatt Earp, sends this message before the final showdown with the bad guys: "You tell 'em I'm comin', and Hell's comin' with me!" It's a great line in a good movie.

For Jesus, the Gospel message was simple. In essence he said, "I've come, and Heaven's come with me." And sure enough, it did.

The Gospel according to Jesus was that he is the one true hope for all humanity. In him, something new and powerful and perfect was happening. And all who believe—giving their full trust to him—experience God in a way that was and is impossible without him.

The most famous verse in all the Bible perfectly encapsulates God's good news. Jesus said this:

> For God so loved the world that he gave his one and only Son, that whoever believes in him shall not perish but have eternal life. (John 3:16 NIV)

The Gospel Jesus preached is the announcement the world and all who inhabit it needed then and still need now. It's no wonder, then, that his first disciples shared the same news gladly and widely.

The Gospel: As Preached by the Early Church

The men and women who walked and talked with Jesus during his lifetime carried on in the Jesus way. They, too, had good news to share. The difference, of course, was that their message did not point to themselves; it pointed to Jesus.

Peter, Jesus' close friend and disciple, gave the first public proclamation of that good news. His speech in Acts chapter two is a long but keen summary of the way they shared the Gospel.

> Fellow Israelites, listen to this: Jesus of Nazareth was a man accredited by God to you by miracles, wonders and signs, which God did among you through him, as you yourselves know. This man was handed over to you by God's deliberate plan and fore-knowledge; and you, with the help of wicked men, put him to death by nailing him to the cross. But God raised him from the dead, freeing him from the agony of death because it was impossible for death to keep its hold on him...
>
> God has raised this Jesus back to life, and we are all witnesses of it. Exalted to the right hand of God, he has received from the Father the promised Holy Spirit and has poured out what you now see and hear...
>
> Therefore let all Israel be assured of this; God has made this Jesus, whom you crucified, both Lord and Messiah. (Acts 2:22-25, 32-33, 36 NIV)

A Jew killed by the Roman occupiers wasn't news. The fact that one of them rose from the dead was. It was *miraculous* news.

But even so, miraculous news isn't necessarily good news. So Peter helped them understand why this news was news of the very best sort.

Jesus, Peter proclaimed, rose from the grave because he is "both Lord and Messiah." In other words, Jesus was God in the flesh (Lord) and the one true King whom God promised to send (Messiah).

Not unlike the message Jesus proclaimed about himself, the good news Peter proclaimed provoked a visceral and powerful response in its hearers. The people, convicted by God through the truth of his good news message, asked "What do we do?"[4]

Peter replied, "Repent and be baptized, every one of you, for the forgiveness of your sins. And you will receive the gift of the Holy Spirit."[5]

And that's what they did. "Those who accepted his message," the Bible goes on to say, "were baptized, and about three thousand were added to their number that day."[6] His message of good news, of forgiveness of sins, of receiving God himself into their lives through the Holy Spirit was powerful and life-changing.

God was doing a new thing, and the good news about Jesus spread like wildfire. The Spirit of God set hearts ablaze with the news that sin's tyranny was over, and reunion with God was possible through this one man, Jesus of Nazareth.

It soon became the very news the early church repeated to one another and shared with all who would listen.

———

So what's the Gospel? It's the good news that Jesus of Nazareth is the Lord of all. He lived, died, and was resurrected according to the Scriptures, now sits at the right hand of God, and one day he will return to establish his perfect kingdom forever.

And because he lived the perfect life with God we are unable to live, and died the sinner's death we deserve to die, we can by faith receive his love, be forgiven of our sinful rebellion, and be reunited with God now and forever more. Hallelujah!

That's the news. That's the announcement. That's the Gospel.

Now that we know what the Gospel is, let's look together at what the Gospel does.

What the Gospel Does

What makes good news good is that it does something. It announces and ignites a change, a shift, a new reality. And nothing could be truer about God's good news.

The Gospel of Jesus Christ does three things: it glorifies God, reunites people with God, and leads any and all into real, authentic human life.

The Gospel Glorifies God

Before we can see how the Gospel glorifies God, we must understand glory.

The Bible's definition of glory is multifaceted. It refers to the "unapproachable and mighty manifestation of [God's] immediate presence" and the "inexpressible beauty and majesty" of God. It also points to the "absolutely pure and terrifying holiness" of God that confronts human sin. Then of course, there is the glory of Christ, which is "especially a consequence of his resurrection from the dead and his ascension to the right hand of the Father."[7]

Last but not least, the Bible calls for all people to give God the glory he's due by surrendering their lives to him and sharing his inexpressible beauty, majesty, holiness, presence, and goodness with others.

Glory describes both what emanates from God and what God is due. He is glorious, and he is worthy of our efforts to glorify him.

In short, glory is the unadulterated specialness of God. God as the Bible describes is unique. He's unlike any other, and he's far better than any other.

So how does the Gospel glorify God? Simply put, the Gospel is the clear message about God's most glorious act.

What God did—reuniting and redeeming all people and creation through the life, death, and resurrection of Jesus Christ— shows his glory in fullest color and brightest display. Every time the Gospel is read, preached, shared, and believed, God is glorified.

Just before his arrest, Jesus prayed for God to be glorified. Talking to the Father, Jesus said, "Father... glorify your Son so he can give glory back to you" and "I brought glory to you here on earth by completing the work you gave me to do."[8]

Jesus' "work"—His perfect human life and sacrificial death— gave God glory, and therefore the Gospel message about his life and work does too. As Jesus said, "Should I pray, 'Father, save me from this hour'? But this is the very reason I came! Father, bring glory to your name."[9]

Several Scripture passages point out that the Gospel glorifies God.[10] One is found in 2 Corinthians 4, where Paul wrote,

> You see, we don't go around preaching about ourselves. We preach that Jesus Christ is Lord, and we ourselves are your servants for Jesus' sake. For God, who said, "Let there be light in the darkness," has made this light shine in our hearts so we could know the glory of God that is seen in the face of Jesus Christ.
>
> We now have this light shining in our hearts, but we ourselves are like fragile clay jars containing this great treasure. This makes it clear that our great power is from God, not from ourselves. (2 Corinthians 4:5-7)

Then in verse fifteen, Paul wrote, "And as God's grace reaches more and more people, there will be great thanksgiving, and God will receive more and more glory."

The good news shows off the goodness of God. He's glorified when we speak the Gospel and when the Gospel's light transforms and shines through us.

The first thing the Gospel does is glorify God. The second thing the Gospel does is bring us back into relationship with God himself.

The Gospel Reunites People with God

One of the most unfortunate misconceptions about Christianity is that the whole point of it is to get to Heaven. Don't get me wrong, I'm certain that Heaven is a wonderful place, and I won't mind being there. But that's not the point.

Rather, the point of Christianity is reunification with God himself.

Religious belief centered on getting to Heaven focuses its adherents on God's stuff, not on God. It misplaces one's hope in the gifts of God rather than in God himself. But God is much too relational, too personal, and too good for just that.

Let's revisit John 17 for what I believe is Jesus' key statement about eternal life. As he spoke with the Father, Jesus said the following, and I don't want you to miss it:

> Now this is eternal life: that they know you, the only true God, and Jesus Christ, whom you have sent. (John 17:3 NIV)

Jesus doesn't think eternal life is some never-ending heavenly existence. The word eternal means without ending *and* without beginning. There is only one being who is eternal, and that is God himself. He has no end or beginning.

Jesus prayed purposefully and passionately for all of us to be united with him, the Father, and each other the same way he is united with the Father.[11]

My friend, the point of Christianity is not going to Heaven. That's but a garnish—an extra dab of goodness on a most spectacular meal.

The point of Christianity is the full reconciliation and reunification of all people to God and each other, now and forever. Divine relationship is the hope of the world and the source of true human life.

Paul wrote it this way in his letter to the new church in Ephesus:

> You lived in this world without God and without hope. But now you have been united with Christ Jesus. Once you were far away from God, but now you have been brought near to him through the blood of Christ.
>
> Now all of us can come to the Father through the same Holy Spirit because of what Christ has done for us. (Ephesians 2:12b-13, 18)

Paul is talking about an actual living, breathing, day-in-and-day-out relationship with the God of the universe. Similarly, when he introduced the Athenian philosophers to God, he said, "For in him we live and move and have our being."[12] He described something far different than just a trip to paradise. He talked of a relationship that fulfills and defines our very existence, life, and being.

The Gospel is the truth about Jesus that makes that possible. It glorifies God and it reunites us with him. Last but not least, the Gospel restores our true humanity, the gateway to real, authentic human life.

The Gospel is the Gateway to Real Human Life

Life as addicted, distracted, aimless, selfish, agonized, sick, and beleaguered people is not what God had in mind. Not even close! Nor did he have in mind a life of constant searching and consuming, fevered pleasure-hunting, and the kind of exploitation and soullessness that characterizes many people on their quest for "happiness."

There's a life so much higher than our stunted highs, deeper than our shallow depths, and richer than our bland monotony.

There's a life that's full—not to capacity with busyness and never-ending task lists, but overflowing with grace and truth, perspective and wisdom, hope and love. A life of abundant joy, peace, patience, kindness, goodness, faithfulness, gentleness, and self-control avails itself because of the good news.

This life—this full and very satisfying life—is not the Gospel, as some seem to claim. But it's one of the *results* of believing and receiving the Gospel.

One of the Apostle Paul's letters is especially useful in helping us understand this concept. His blessing in Ephesians describes what happens when we receive and trust the Gospel announcement.

> Christ will make his home in your hearts as you trust in him. Your roots will grow down into God's love and keep you strong. And may you have the power to understand, as all God's people should, how wide, how long, how high, and how deep his love is. May you experience the love of Christ, though it is too great to understand fully. Then you will be made complete with all the fullness of life and power that comes from God. (Ephesians 3:17-19)

Once we grasp the Gospel and believe it, God begins to make us complete "with all the fullness and power that comes from God." *All* the fullness and power to be the people God designed us to be.

Jesus said it this way:

> If you try to hang on to your life, you will lose it. But if you give up your life for my sake and for the sake of the good news, you will save it. (Mark 8:35)

And *that's* the point. Receiving the Gospel isn't about a ticket to some ethereal afterlife. It's about unity with God. It's about being saved from eternal separation from the fountainhead of love and life. It's about being rescued from our sinful self-implosion so we can finally know God, be welcomed into his family, and grow into the fullness of real life with him.

———

The Westminster Shorter Catechism, written in 1646 by English and Scottish theologians, begins with this:

Question: What is the chief end of man?

Answer: Man's chief end is to glorify God, and to enjoy him forever.[13]

This is what the Gospel does. It glorifies God, and through it the Spirit of God leads us into relationship with the Father and into true human life. The Gospel provides the way for us to enjoy our good God forever.

It is, then, *very* good news. And I don't know about you, but when I know something that good, I want to share it with everyone.

Sharing the Message

Bible scholar and theologian D.A. Carson wrote,

Because the gospel is news, good news... it is to be announced; that is what one does with news. The essential heraldic element in preaching is bound up with the fact that the core message is not a code of ethics to be debated, still less a list of aphorisms to be admired and pondered, and certainly not a systematic theology to be outlined and schematized. Though it properly grounds ethics, aphorisms, and systematics, it is none of these three: it is news, good news, and therefore must be publicly announced.[14]

Carson is right. Regardless of whether or not you consider yourself to be a preacher, there's good news to be shared.

Remember how you texted, posted, tweeted, called, and shouted to your friends, family, and colleagues when your alma mater won the national championship, when you got engaged, or when you landed your dream job? I do.

Heck, I remember stopping by half my co-workers' offices just to tell them somebody put fresh donuts in the coffee lounge.

The thing about good news is that it gets shared. If it's seriously good—for us and for others we know and love—then it's difficult *not* to share.

No other good, delightful, fun, important, or helpful news compares to the truth that human beings, who deserve nothing from God, can be restored to him and become full participants in his restoration project for the world. This news is *the* best news!

I hope this review of the Gospel will do for you what it's done for me. It's renewed my wonder and worship for God, and it's refreshed my desire to share it with any who have yet to catch wind of God's life-saving message.

In the "How I Practice" section at the end of this chapter, I describe how I go about sharing God's good news. I hope it will help you. But in the end, it is not a method that makes us share; it's our belief that the Gospel truly is good news—news that we personally need and benefit from—that compels us to share.

So what do you think? Is the Gospel good news to you? Have you shared it with anyone lately?

If not, perhaps it's because you need to preach it to yourself again first. The Gospel is good news for this dying world, but it is also vital news for *your* weary soul. It's news that brings rest to all who hear it, including you.

Preach to Yourself

Psalm 42 is a beautiful poem about the author's deep desire for encounters with God, and it's a heart-wrenching reflection on his debilitating depression as he encounters the world. Give it a read and see if your expressions and feelings ever match his.

> As the deer longs for streams of water,
>   so I long for you, O God.
>   I thirst for God, the living God.
>   When can I go and stand before him?
>   Day and night I have only tears for food,
>   while my enemies continually taunt me, saying,
>   "Where is this God of yours?"
>   My heart is breaking
>   as I remember how it used to be:
>   I walked among the crowds of worshipers,
>   leading a great procession to the house of God,
>   singing for joy and giving thanks
>   amid the sound of a great celebration! (Psalm 42:1-4)

Do you recognize his desire for God? Do you resonate with his sorrow and heartbreak?

Anyone who says the Bible doesn't face real life head-on is wrong. The psalmist's true heart and the difficulty of life are on full display here.

He *longs* for God, yet day and night he is depressed, anxious, and worried. He *longs* for the days when he and his community sang for joy in worship as they travelled together to the house of God, yet his heart breaks because that's no longer his reality.

But instead of wallowing in worry, he employs a powerful practice that instructs and helps us today: He preaches to himself.

Look at the next verse in this psalm:

> Why am I discouraged?
>   Why is my heart so sad?
>   I will put my hope in God!

I will praise him again—
my Savior and my God! (Psalm 42:5-6a)

The psalmist takes an honest look at two things: his circumstances and his God. Then, in light of the former, he preaches to himself about the latter.

Martin Lloyd-Jones, a Welsh-born doctor, minister, and author wrote,

> Have you realized that most of your unhappiness in life is due to the fact that you are listening to yourself instead of talking to yourself?.... Now this man's treatment [in Psalm 42] was this; instead of allowing this self to talk to him, he starts talking to himself, "Why art thou cast down, O my soul?" he asks. His soul had been repressing him, crushing him. So he stands up and says: "Self, listen for a moment, I will speak to you"...
>
> The main art in the matter of spiritual living is to know how to handle yourself. You have to take yourself in hand, you have to address yourself, preach to yourself, question yourself. You must say to your soul: "Why art thou cast down"–what business have you to be disquieted? You must turn on yourself... and say to yourself: "Hope thou in God"–instead of muttering in this depressed, unhappy way. And then you must go on to remind yourself of God, who God is, and what God is and what God has done, and what God has pledged himself to do.[15]

Now *that's* preaching to yourself.

Even if you're not currently in a spiritual depression, Lloyd-Jones's interpretation of the psalmist is a good one. Preaching the Gospel to ourselves is a vital part of a Christian life.

Too many mistakenly believe that mature Christians eventually move beyond the Gospel to deeper and wider theological truths. But this is false. *There are no Bible truths wider or deeper than the Gospel.*

We misconceive the Gospel when we think of it only as an onramp to faith. The Gospel is the road on which every Christian travels to get to every place God desires for him to go. The good news about Jesus sustains any and every believer any and every day of her life.

The Gospel's depths will never be fully plumbed. Its width will never be fully grasped. Its height will never be fully reached. Even the Apostle Paul, the greatest of all Christian theologians, knew this.

Paul's Sermon to Himself

Romans 7 is a lot like Psalm 42 in that it gives us an honest and vulnerable look into the soul of a Christian saint. Even the Apostle Paul struggled with sin and doubt and frustration.

In the heart of his letter to the church in Rome, he admitted his weakness.

> I know that nothing good lives in me, that is, in my sinful nature. I want to do what is right, but I can't. I want to do what is good, but I don't. I don't want to do what is wrong, but I do it anyway. (Romans 7:18-19)

Then, in a moment of self-reflection and exasperation, he concluded with these words:

> Oh, what a miserable person I am! Who will free me from this life that is dominated by sin and death? (Romans 7:24)

The most influential missionary, church-planter, preacher, and theologian in Christian history was broken, just like you and me. And he *knew* it. And he wrote about it.

I, for one, am glad he did. Through his written words we see Paul's inner struggle. We also learn his personal remedy. In the face of his spiritual depression, he gave a stern but freeing lecture to his own soul. He pointed himself back to Jesus Christ, the subject of the Gospel he so often preached, with these simple words:

> Thank God! The answer is in Jesus Christ our Lord. (Romans 7:25)

Then he penned Romans chapter eight, one of his most magisterial chapters of all. It beautifully summarizes the glorious hope we find in Jesus through the Gospel. It's moving to know that Paul wrote it as much for himself as for the Roman church. And by God's grace, we still have it today.

Do yourself a favor and read it sometime very soon. Let it serve as a reminder of God's love, the Gospel message, and why it's so valuable to share with others and preach to ourselves.

What Happens if You Don't Share the Gospel?

In Romans 10:9-13, Paul wrote out the Gospel in its beautiful simplicity. Then in verse 14, he wrote this:

> But how can they call on him to save them unless they believe in him? And how can they believe in him if they have never heard about him? And how can they hear about him unless someone tells them?

If you and I don't share the Gospel, who will? We might assume that because church buildings still stand in every American town that everyone knows the Gospel. But it's not true. And it's becoming less and less true as the decades press on and we become an increasingly post-Christian culture.

If we don't share, people won't hear. If they don't hear, they can't believe. If people don't believe, they will never be reunited with the God who made and loves them.

God made the Church to continue the work Jesus began. Sharing the Gospel is integral to that purpose and mission.

Now what if you don't preach the Gospel to yourself? If you only listen and never talk to yourself, the voice of self-deception, the sway of family history, the seduction of sinful passion, or the rigor of religious dogma will push you away from a life of true freedom, confidence, joy, and purpose.

If you don't internalize the Gospel for yourself, you will eventually live a life of either license or legalism.

License is the belief that nothing is wrong, that salvation (and thus a Savior) is unnecessary, and that it doesn't matter how you live. It's the idea that you're the captain of your own ship, and the God you imagine does not, cannot, and will not disapprove of you or what you do. It's the functional belief that God is not real or is not remotely interested.

By contrast, legalism is a brand of religious practice that makes our good standing with God solely up to us. The legalist must strike the right balance of perfect action, pure motives, and full commitment, or God will reject him or her. It's the functional belief that *you* are your savior.

Similarly, legalism also makes you the captain of your own ship, but dissimilarly there's a God who does, can, and will always disapprove of you. The whole goal of legalism is to be good enough or religious enough to earn his favor.

Thankfully, the Gospel of Jesus Christ shatters both heresies.

What Happens if You Do Share the Gospel?

The very best thing that happens when we share the Gospel is that God is glorified. It happens every single time we lovingly and courageously share.

The second-best thing that happens is that others are given the opportunity to be reunited with God, filled with his Spirit, and empowered to begin living their real lives. Though it doesn't happen every time, there is nothing more thrilling than when someone takes that opportunity and discovers true hope and freedom in Jesus.

There are also enormous benefits when we remind ourselves of the Gospel. Each time we do, we combat the lies Satan whispers and the ones we often repeat to ourselves.

When we grasp the goodness of the good news, we enjoy freedom that's far richer than license and a spirituality that's far better than legalism. Every single day, the voice of our sinful nature[16] and the ways of our secular world speak passionately and persuasively about living only for pleasure or attempting to earn our salvation.

It is only the Gospel of Jesus Christ and the Spirit of God within us that shut that voice up and provide the life-giving relief we so desperately need.

As I wrote in Rule #5, Join the Church, you ought not be the only Gospel preacher in your life. You need brothers and sisters in God's family to remind you of the Gospel and the freedom song it sings.

Finally, the additional benefit of preaching the Gospel to yourself is that doing so equips you to preach it to others. You don't become a faithful witness of the Gospel because you memorized a message but rather because you understand and live in the eternal light of it.

Experience the life that only Jesus provides, and you'll waste no time sharing it with others. Preach to yourself regularly and you'll gain the confidence needed to share with others regularly too.

How I Practice Rule #12

God answers one prayer of mine more than any other. And he always answers it with a "yes!" Want to know what that prayer is?

When I ask him to provide an opportunity for me to share the

Gospel with someone, he *never* fails to provide one (often within the week).

Just two weeks before writing this, I prayed with a group of friends for God to provide occasions to share the Gospel.

Four days later, while getting a spot of skin cancer removed from my forehead, the physician made small talk by asking about my interest and hobbies. I told him about this book, and it sparked a conversation about God and life. It was the moment for which I prayed. And I took it.

On more than one occasion, however, I've failed to take those God-given opportunities. It's unbelievably selfish of me, but my failure to take gospel opportunities never stops God from answering my prayer and providing them.

The first spiritual practice for Share the Gospel is to regularly ask God for opportunities to do so. The second practice is to take them when he does.

Before you get anxious about what that looks like, take a deep breath and realize that in no time at all (if you actually pray and pay attention), God will start by pointing out opportunities to personally recall the gospel before you share it with others.

When that chance comes up, don't miss it. Like the psalmist and Paul, your wayward heart needs the reminder.

Similarly, ask God for chances to share the Gospel with someone else. The moments will come, and they will be far more organic than you might imagine.

A family member will open up about their troubles in a way they never have before.

A neighbor will linger at your door longer than usual.

Your child will become more curious than normal about the things of God.

Someone might even ask you why you go to church.

However the God-given gospel opportunity arises, take it.

———

The Gospel is the amazing news that God loves us and his creation so much that he gave himself to rescue, redeem, and be reunited with every bit of it.

It's an announcement so good that it's shocking and almost unbelievable. But when you allow it to seep into your heart, refusing to let your familiarity with it ruin its power, it proves to be the very best of good news.

This incredible news is for us to receive and trust and share so that any and all may enjoy a relationship with God and experience the wholeness, joy, purpose, meaning, and freedom that God alone —through his gospel—provides.

May you and I return again and again to this truth, soak in its goodness, and then start preaching!

EPILOGUE

"These exercises are not laws that bind us, nor are they practices we can neglect if we want to grow in our life with God and with one another. They stretch us and awaken us to the leading of the Spirit without becoming a recipe with a predictable outcome."
—Dr. James Bryan Smith

Finishing a book like this is kind of like being handed a huge set of blueprints for a sprawling new home. It offers a beautiful and compelling sketch of what's possible, but it leaves all but the most well-trained builders grasping at straws. Most of us would stare blankly at the construction plans and wonder, *How and where do I even begin?*

Whether you're a new follower of Jesus, trying to reengage your faith, or looking to mature and deepen your growing life in God, there's much to consider in *12 Rules for a Christian Life.*

The Rules—like a set of blueprints—are the guide to a well-built life. But if you're like me, you could use a recommendation for how to begin and an accessible list of reminders about all you've read.

The former is the goal of this epilogue. It's written to encourage and equip you for taking the next step. The latter is the goal of the Appendix. It will provide a keen summary of each Rule so you can refresh your memory now or whenever needed.

First, the epilogue. Here's how to get started with these new rhythms for your real life with God.

Jesus, Pick the Rule

You've read the Rules and learned from my practices, but now it's time for you to adopt them as your own and start building the life God invites you to move into. But how in the world do you know which Rules to begin with? You've got the full set of blueprints, but how do you begin building?

I believe with deep conviction that your next step is to adopt and practice *three* of the Rules.

Why three? And which ones?

I'm glad you asked.

I encourage you to commit right now to Rule #1 and Rule #2. Take time to re-read both chapters together as one: Fight for Space and Listen to Jesus.

Then, I would challenge you to let Jesus pick the third Rule for you when he believes you're good and ready. Here's why:

In our busy, distracting, and maddening world, Rule #1—Fight For Space—is almost always the first step. We have to make space to connect (or reconnect) with God.

Then Rule #2—Listen To Jesus—is how you step into the real, open, obedient, and reciprocal relationship with God that he desires and designed for you.

Commit to those two Rules, and Jesus will take it from there, pointing you to whichever Rule he wants you to engage next.

He may tell you that your next step is to Name Your Idols. He may tell you to Join the Church. He may help you Remember Who You Are or bring to your mind the name of one person he wants you to Share the Gospel with.

In time, he will identify a Rule for you, invite you to read about it again, then ask you to practice it. But first, he wants you to start where he started: He fought for space and listened to the Father. Then he obediently, faithfully, purposefully, and enthusiastically did what the Father said.

Now it's your turn. It's *our* turn.

Recently in my own space with Jesus, I realized God was speaking to me through the Scriptures and various circumstances. He said, "Share the Gospel, Chris. There are people all around you who need to hear it." And as I obey and look for opportunities to live out that Rule, God provides them.

I wonder... what will he say to you? Are you ready to Fight For Space, Listen to Jesus, and find out? There's a third Rule with your name on it, and it's the step God wants you to take as you go all-in on life with him.

Bonus Rule #13: Go All In

In this book's introduction, under the heading "Losing is Saving, Saving is Losing," I quoted verses from Mark's Gospel that read like this:

> Calling the crowd to join his disciples, he said, "If any of you wants to be my follower, you must give up your own way, take up your cross, and follow me. If you try to hang on to your life, you will lose it. But if you give up your life for my sake and for the sake of the good news, you will save it. And what do you benefit if you gain the whole world but lose your own soul? Is anything worth more than your soul?" (Mark 8:34-37)

Until only a few years ago, I was confused by Jesus' words "take up your cross" in verse thirty-four. I struggled to understand what they meant for Christians like me in twenty-first century America.

Did he mean that his followers needed to be *willing* to die for him? Or to *actually* die for him? Was he telling his faithful they would suffer physical pain, social ostracization, psychological torment, or public humiliation? Because that's most certainly what he endured when he took up his cross.

Recently, the Spirit of God answered my question. Jesus' words "take up your cross" are not words about torture, death, or humiliation. They are words about devotion.

In the Garden of Gethsemane, Jesus asked the Father if there was any other way to redeem humanity than by bearing all the world's sin and shame and being put to death on a Roman cross. In the end, the answer was no, and Jesus' absolute devotion was on full display when he responded, "I want your will to be done, not mine."[1]

Because of what God was doing for us, Jesus lived—and died—fully devoted to him.

Now, because of what God has done for us, Jesus calls us to live —and die—fully devoted to him.

Jesus went all in. And he lived true human life because of it. So *that* is my final encouragement, or final Rule, for you.

Go. All. In.

Your greatest life is the one God made you to live, lived the way God made it to be lived. When you go all-in with God, through Jesus, by the power of the Holy Spirit, you will begin to live and enjoy the beautiful life God made for you.

These 12 Rules are rules for *life*—a Christian life—the only life there truly is for any person, anywhere, at any time.

Fight for Space.
Listen to Jesus.
Read the Bible Slowly.
Become a Mystic.
Join the Church.
Don't Just Sing There.
Give Yourself Away.
Redefine Love.
Remember Who You Are.
Name Your Idols.
Embrace Your Suffering.
Share the Gospel.

Do the first two. Let Jesus pick the third. Then Go All In. Your real life is waiting. Don't miss it.

MORE FOR THE JOURNEY

The 12 Rules Group Guides

Rule #5, Join the Church, reminded us that God made us to live life with others. These Rules then, are most faithfully lived and fruitfully experienced with fellow travelers.

To that end, I'm excited to tell you about the *12 Rules for a Christian Life: Group Guides.*

Each Group Guide—one for each of the Rules—includes additional biblical perspective, other spiritual practices, and thought-provoking questions for group conversation.

The *12 Rules for a Christian Life: Group Guides* will help you and your friends further understand the practices and priorities of Jesus and integrate them into your lives as you follow him *together.*

Choose a Group Guide for any single Rule or work through them all to create a six-month group experience with friends, family, classmates, small group participants, neighbors, or church leaders.

Once published, you can find the Group Guides at www.ChrisGreer.com.

Updates, Resources, and a Gift

I also invite you to visit www.Chris-Greer.com for additional books, the 12 Rules for a Christian Life Podcast, and other free resources for living your real life in Jesus.

When you sign up for my email updates at www.Chris-Greer.com, I'll send you a free "thank you" gift for reading.

Subscribers will also learn how to join my Advance Reader Team. Advance Readers receive a copy of future books ahead of publication to provide me helpful feedback and to help spread the word about the new book.

God willing, all of this will help you along the journey.

Help the Book Help Others

If this book was meaningful or helpful, would you please write a review at Amazon? I read and appreciate every review.

Would you also consider telling a friend or posting on social media about the book?

Honest reviews and personal recommendations are the best ways to help others find and read *12 Rules for a Christian Life* and encourage independent authors like me in the work we do.

Thank you,
    Chris

ACKNOWLEDGMENTS

"All of us, at some time or other, need help. Whether we're giving or receiving help, each one of us has something valuable to bring to this world."
—Fred Rogers

The quality of anyone's life—like that of any one book—is contingent on the selfless participation of others. The following friends and family have added to the quality of my life and therefore the quality of this book, and I owe each a debt of gratitude.

———

Kerry: Your steadfast relationship with God and your unwavering love and courage is the backbone of our family. Your name should be included on the cover of this book because without your belief and encouragement in me, it would not exist. You are a gift, and I love you.

Jacob and Emma: Your voices, your energy, and your hugs are fuel for my soul. May your enthusiasm for life become your enthusiasm for Jesus. And yes, I will play Legos and babies with you.

Mom, Dad, Andrew, Trey, and Stephanie: Thank you for helping me remember that being a Greer means being a follower and friend of Jesus. I've always needed your example, and I still do.

AK, Susan, Grammy, and Mor Mor: Thank you for always serving and cheering for us. The Greers love you.

Whitlocks, Etters, Neals, and Dymnas: Thank you for agreeing to "do life" with us. It's so good to be in community with you. Let's keep it up.

Patrick, Fucci, Afam, Kyle, Michael G., and Sister Elle: Thank you for your friendship. Distance and time does not diminish the value or impact of it.

George: Thank you for helping me remember that the Gospel is the only message to preach. Your mentorship and friendship mean the world to me.

Stan: Thank you for helping me get a start in real book-writing. If I write half as many books, half as well as you, I'll consider this thing a success.

People of Fellowship North: Thank you for embracing and encouraging our family. It's an honor to serve with you.

People of St. Andrews Presbyterian: Thank you for your hospitality and generosity of spirit. It was an honor to cut my teeth with you.

Ben: Thank you for being a brother in the faith I didn't know I had and for making the book better.

Bill: Thank you for applying your keen eye to this manuscript. You've still got it.

Advance Readers: Thank you for jumping in first and providing your honest feedback. It was a big help.

And to you: Thank you for "picking up a copy" of *12 Rules for a Christian Life* and giving it a read. I pray God uses the reading of it for his good purposes in your life, just as he has used the writing of it for his good purposes in mine.

———

Maranatha, Lord Jesus, Maranatha.

APPENDIX

"A spiritual discipline is any activity that can help you gain power to live life as Jesus taught and modeled it."
—John Ortberg

Need a simple reminder of what each Rule in *12 Rules for a Christian Life* is all about? Here they are in a nutshell.

Use these reminders about each rule and accompanying practice to jog your memory, jump start your own practices, or help you talk with others about *12 Rules for a Christian Life.*

Rule #1: Fight for Space

There is a reason why this is Rule #1. We live crowded, busy, and overwhelming lives, but God is neither noisy nor in a hurry. He longs to gift us with rest, deep breaths, and a life overwhelmed with his goodness rather than our culture's mediocrity.

However, God does not force himself, or his gifts, on us.

Although everything real in life begins with his initiation, we must diligently carve out space to respond to his grace. Regardless of whether it is extended, sabbath, daily, or prompted space, we must fight for unburdened and undistracted time to simply be with God.

Once we prioritize him, the floodgates open, and we begin to taste and see that the Lord is good,[1] and we reap the benefits of the remaining Rules.

Practice – Fight for Space with The Daily Pause and First Fridays.

Rule #2: Listen to Jesus

In his book, *Whole Prayer,* Walter Wangerin describes communication with God as a four-step process. He writes, "Prayer is made up of four acts, four discrete parts, two of which are ours, two of which are God's...

- First, we speak,
- while, second, God listens.
- Third, God speaks,
- while, fourth, we listen."[2]

He goes on to point out that many of us stop at step number two.

Lots of us talk, assuming God listens, then we stop our prayers before allowing God a turn to speak. Thus, we need Rule #2—Listen to Jesus.

The Bible makes it clear that God communicates—by the Spirit of Jesus—primarily through the Bible, but also through desires, doors, dreams, people, promptings, pain, and peace. God is a communicative God who desires his people to know him, recognize the ways he speaks, and listen carefully to him.

Listening to Jesus is the heart and soul of real human life, which is life with a personal and loving God. And he has much to say if we choose to tune in.

Practice – Listen to Jesus by prioritizing silence, reading scripture, and journaling.

Rule #3: Read the Bible…Slowly

It's impossible to live the way of Jesus and discover true human life apart from reading the Bible. It's God's Word to us and for us, and it's authoritative for life and faith.

Unfortunately, our Western educational training teaches us to approach the Bible—and every other book we read—for one of two purposes: entertainment (fiction) or information (non-fiction). But the Bible, while both vastly entertaining and incredibly informative, is neither a novel nor a textbook. It's far more, much better, and drastically different from all other texts.

The Bible is God's living Word. It's alive and active[3], fully inspired by God himself to lead you and me in the life we are born to live.[4]

Rule #3 helps us to read God's Word not just for information but for *transformation*. This Rule leads us to engage with God through his written Word in deeper, better, and slower ways, helping us understand the text, find ourselves in God's story, and listen to Jesus.

Practice – Read the Bible Slowly and listen to God through the practice, *lectio divina.*

Rule #4: Become a Mystic

Rationalism is the belief that everything real can be diagnosed, measured, and repeated, while emotionalism is the belief that what is most real is what is most deeply felt.

Rationalism paves the way to a less than fully human life while emotionalism leads to isolation and loneliness. Neither humanistic belief system is God's best, which is why he gave us something far better.

Reconciliation with God is a far more miraculous—and myste-rious—spiritual reality than either rationalism or emotionalism. A relationship with God through Jesus, by his Spirit, is a mystical union between Creator and creation, supernatural and natural, divine and human.

This reality is the source of the miracle of life and every one of life's miracles. And to be fully human is to realize what the priest and philosopher Pierre Teilhard de Chardin did. He wrote, "We are not human beings having spiritual experiences: We are spiritual beings having human experiences."[5]

Practices – Become a Mystic by remembering mystical moments with God.

Rule #5: Join the Church

One of the great heresies on the lips of some American Chris-tians is, "I don't need the church to be in relationship with Jesus." This statement reveals the influence of Western individualism more than it does a biblical understanding of Christianity.

Community, relationship, union, and togetherness with God and his people are paramount for life as a Christ follower.

For all eternity past, God has existed in perfect community—one God in three persons: Father, Son, and Spirit. He never has been and never will be alone. So what makes any of us think that receiving his grace and living as his child is an individualistic reality?

The triune God designed human beings in his image, to live in his way, within a community of loving relationships. Christians who desire to experience real life in Christ do so within a commu-nity. They join God's church by participating, committing, identify-ing, and extending themselves with God's people. In so doing, they discover ad share real life.

Practice – Join the Church by praying for and trying out gospel-centered friendship.

Rule #6: Don't Just Sing There

People used the proper noun "Google" to describe the action of searching for things on the internet so often that it is now included in the English dictionary as a verb. Popular usage transformed its meaning.

And so it is with the word "worship." Because of overuse, many American Christians think "worship" is little more than singing on Sundays or a subgenre of Christian music. Fortunately, the Bible remedies our ignorance about the true meaning of this important word.

Biblical worship, as per Romans 12:1-2, is the full surrender of one's life in complete and total devotion to God alone.

Worship is a way of living, not simply a kind of singing. And we shortchange ourselves, and the watching world, when we Christians so narrowly define it.

Singing to God can be a beautiful and biblical expression of our devotion to him, but what God deserves and demands, for our and others' sake, is far more. True human life is found when we turn our entire lives over to the One who created us, loves us, and redeemed us.

Practice – Don't Just Sing There by changing the way you speak and trying something different this Sunday.

Rule #7: Give Yourself Away

One of the ways to describe the fundamental ideology of our culture is with the phrase, "I am my own." It's this belief—held by virtually everyone in the postmodern West—that fuels our obsession with privacy and independence.

Yes, God has given you the privilege of choice, and with it you can choose a life independent of him. But God yearns for us to have a mentality that aligns with reality, and he knows—and his

Word declares—the truth: You were made by him and for him. You are not your own.

This actuality humbles us. We all want to run our own lives, but what too few people realize, including Christians, is that life is sweetest when you come to terms with the fact that you are a creation and child of the King, and you will live your best life fully yielded to him in the love and service of others.

God is glorified, his kingdom comes, and we can serve others in profound ways when we live according to our design to give ourselves away rather than hoarding ourselves for ourselves. In God's economy, when we generously give our lives away, we find them.[6]

Practice – Give Your Life Away by meditating on Luke 15:25-37 and committing to serve someone this week.

Rule #8: Redefine Love

God's love is not the same as our world's. Our world says that love is designed to affirm who you believe you are, at all costs, in all situations, no matter the outcome. In stark contrast, true love—God's love—is designed to *change* who you are.

God loves us enough to tell us we could never merit his love. And God loves us so much that even though we are undeserving, he relentlessly pursues us and loves us anyway. It's so good and gracious that it boggles the mind.

God's love simultaneously shows us who we really are and enables us to become who he knows we can become. But in our overly sensitive, narcissistic, self-gratifying world, God's discipline and correction—both vital aspects of his generous and bettering love—feel like an affront. Yet his conviction and instruction are designed to perfect us, not perturb us.

Unfortunately, our secular society is duped by a definition of love that leaves us as we are, muddled in our own self-definition.

Praise God that he is far better to us than we could ever be to ourselves. He provides love that never settles for leaving us where we are but moves us deeper into a regenerative relationship with him.

Only those humble enough to redefine their understanding of love will align with his original definition and discover real life within his transforming love.

Practice – Redefine Love by opening yourself to honest spiritual feedback from God and a trusted Jesus follower.

Rule #9: Remember Who You Are

God created you. God knows you. God loves you. And God even *likes* you.

For some—maybe you—this is difficult to believe. You certainly didn't create yourself, and at times you don't really know, love, or like yourself.

When we don't remember who God says we are, we too easily define ourselves by, well, *ourselves*. And that definition is always cast under the influence of our cultural milieu.

Your family of origin plays a massive role in how you understand yourself. Your culture—be it American or another, urban or rural, black, white, Hispanic, or Asian, educated or not, wealthy or poor, Democrat or Republican, popular or unpopular—shapes your view of yourself, for good or for ill.

But true human life is experienced only when we rely on the definition provided by the Creator. And the Bible is clear: Your Creator knows you, loves you, and likes you. It is from the foundation of a stable identity in Christ that Christians live the life they were made to live.

Practice – Remember Who You Are by identifying your limiting beliefs and God's liberating truths.

Rule #10: Name Your Idols

You don't have to be religious to recognize that all human beings worship something. Regardless of persuasion, everyone devotes their life to a person, idea, pursuit, feeling, or God/god.

There is only one God who gives life, and everything else is a cheap replacement that steals true life. This is why repentance— the practice of turning our hearts, souls, and minds to God and away from whatever is *not* God—is a core task of the Christian life.

Unfortunately, idols pop up in our lives on more than one occasion. The objects of your affection and recipients of your devotion will differ significantly in your teen years and in your twilight years, in your marriage years and in your single years, in your working years and in your retirement years.

Therefore, each of us must constantly recognize, repent, reject, and replace all of the non-God objects, ideas, and relationships that tempt us away from him.

Thankfully, as we grow and mature, this process becomes easier, and we can put a variety of potential idols to bed. The true Christian life is honest about the persuasive pretenders that want to stand in the place of the King of kings.

Boldly name your idols so you can reject them at every turn, and you will live more fully into the one true life that the one true God provides.

Practice – Name Your Idols by reviewing your priorities through the Daily Examen, and confess your idols to another Jesus-follower.

Rule #11: Embrace Your Suffering

Suffering is the great common denominator. Everyone must endure it at one point or another. God's future for his perfect creation is pain-free,[7] but until Jesus returns and all human sin is eliminated, suffering will be our constant companion.

When we embrace God in our darkest moments, he matures us, frees us, and sets us on a mission. When we lean into God as the flood waters rise, we experience the Savior, see the world clearly, and step into deeper relationship with our Lord.

Some of what is possible because of suffering is not possible without it, and the great Redeemer invites us to face the pain knowing we can and will find him in it.

Heartache and hardship are the terrible realities of a world broken by sin. But God is so good that the existence of suffering does not thwart his plan. In fact, God redeems suffering for his glory, others' good, and our joy if we patiently allow him to work through our pain.

Practice – Embrace Your Suffering by praying the Psalms and praising God in whatever circumstances you're in.

Rule #12: Share the Gospel

The best message any human has ever heard is called the Gospel.

It's the Bible's good news that God's promised Messiah, Jesus of Nazareth, lived a perfect life that no other human has lived, he died the kind of death every one of us sinners deserves to die, and God miraculously raised him from the dead three days later. And now this Jesus, the proven Son of God, sits in glory at the right hand of God the Father and will one day return in glory to renew all his creation.

When we trust this message—believing by faith that Christ died in our place—and confess and repent of our sin, we are reunited with God and filled by his Holy Spirit, who leads us in living true human life.

Jesus boldly taught this good news, and his first followers bravely touted it. Since then, God entrusts every Jesus-follower with the responsibility and privilege of sharing the Gospel with a needy world.[8]

And when I say, "Every person on the planet needs this news," that includes *you*. The Bible reminds us that preaching the Gospel to ourselves is also a much-needed practice. After all, trusting the Gospel is both what makes you a Christian and *keeps* you a Christian. The good news about Jesus Christ is the truth that starts your Christian life and sustains it.

Unfortunately, we are prone to forget it amid the pressures and problems, fears and failures, maladies and mistakes of life. Yet in every moment it is the Gospel alone that we *must* remember.

So out of obedience to God and necessity for life, love for our neighbors and longing for ourselves, we share the Gospel of Jesus Christ with one and all.

Practice – Share the Gospel by intentionally praying for, waiting for, then acting on opportunities to tell others the good news about Jesus.

NOTES

Introduction

1. https://www.pewforum.org/2019/10/17/in-u-s-decline-of-christianity-continues-at-rapid-pace/
2. See John 10:10
3. Malcolm Gladwell - *Outliers: The Story of Success* - p.31
4. https://practicingtheway.org/unhurrying-with-a-rule-of-life/workbook
5. See Mark 12:28
6. https://www.barna.com/research/changing-state-of-the-church/
7. See Matthew 5:17-18
8. See John 3:2
9. See John 3:3
10. See John 17:2
11. I believe in the biblical, orthodox Christian doctrine of the Trinity which states that God is a unique, triune being. God the Father, God the Son (Jesus), and God the Spirit (Holy Spirit) are three distinct persons of the one true God. The Father, Jesus, and Holy Spirit are different and distinct from one another, but each is God. So while the Father is not the Son, the Son is not the Spirit, and the Spirit is neither the Father nor the Son, all three are God.

    There are theologians, authors, and pastors who explain this miraculous reality far better than I, and I happily recommend them to you. You might start with *Theology for the Community of God* by Stanley Grenz, *The Deep Things of God,* by Fred Sanders, and *Fire and Wind* by my friend, Stan Jantz.

    In summary, I believe God, Jesus, and the Holy Spirit are God, so I use their names interchangeably (though this may annoy some folks).
12. See John 13:17 and Matthew 7:24-27

1. Fight For Space

1. Mark 1:34
2. Mark 1:35
3. Mark 1:36-37
4. Luke 5:16
5. Matthew 4:1-11, Mark 1:12-13, Luke 4:1-13
6. Luke 6:12
7. Matthew 14:23

8. Luke 5:16
9. Luke 22:39
10. Matthew 14:13
11. Matthew 14:23
12. Matthew 26:36
13. Mark 9:29
14. Luke 11:1
15. https://www.mhanational.org/issues/state-mental-health-america
16. https://www.barna.com/research/mental-health-next-gen/
17. See Matthew 11:28-30

2. Listen To Jesus

1. www.SeekWell.org and www.TheDailyRhythm.org
2. "He Lives" - Alfred H. Ackley
3. See John 7:38
4. John 10:10b
5. See John 5:30 and 8:28 NASB
6. John 6:38
7. See Luke 19:10
8. See Matthew 26:36-45 and John 6:30b
9. John 9:7
10. John 10:3b, 4b
11. Mark Batterson - *Whisper* - pgs 63-169
12. Psalm 37:4-5
13. Matthew 6:24
14. John 10:10b
15. John 10:14-15a
16. John 10:10
17. 1 Kings 19:12b
18. See Matthew 7:24 and John 13:17

3. Read The Bible...Slowly

1. John Mark Comer - *Ruthless Elimination of Hurry* - pg 33 (cited from Kerby Anderson - *Technology and Social Trends: A biblical Point of View* - pg 102)
2. Nicholas G. Carr - *The Shallows: What The Internet Is Doing To Our Brains* - pg 7
3. Matthew 3:2
4. Isaiah 40:3
5. Matthew 4:1
6. Matthew 4:3

7. Matthew 4:3
8. See John 10:10
9. Psalm 119:11
10. See Jeremiah 15:16 and Ezekiel 3:1-3
11. Robert J. Mulholland - *Shaped by the Word* - pg 54
12. See John 1:1-5
13. 1 Timothy 6:19
14. Jeremiah 29:13
15. See John 4:23

4. Become A Mystic

1. Mark 8:27-28
2. Mark 8:29
3. See Mark 8:29-33
4. See 2 Peter 1:16-18
5. Matt Chandler - Village Church Podcast, Matt Chandler, Flower Mound - episode from March 22, 2020
6. Hans Christian Andersen - *Shorter Tales*
7. See 1 Corinthians 12:12-31
8. See Acts 1:8, 1 Corinthians 6:19
9. See John 15:1-8
10. Matthew 6:10
11. 2 Corinthians 5:17
12. See 1 John 4
13. See Mark 9
14. See 2 Kings 6
15. See Acts 16:18
16. Quote regularly attributed to Pierre Teilhard de Chardin, the French Jesuit priest and philosopher (1881 - 1955)
17. Ephesians 5:18
18. Find our more about Alan Fadling and his important and helpful work at www.UnhurriedLiving.com.

5. Join The Church

1. https://www.psychologytoday.com/us/blog/talking-about-men/201707/is-increase-in-individualism-damaging-our-mental-health
2. See "Social Dilemma"—a Netflix original documentary
3. https://www.nimh.nih.gov/health/statistics/suicide.shtml
   https://www.medicalnewstoday.com/articles/322877#What-is-anxiety?
   https://www.the-sun.com/news/1487147/social-media-suicides-self-harm-

netflix-social-dilemma/
4. Matthew 4:19
5. See John 1:40-41
6. Luke 5:10b
7. Luke 5:11
8. Matthew 16:18
9. John 13:35
10. https://www.biblestudytools.com/lexicons/greek/nas/ekklesia.html
11. {$NOTE_LABEL} https://www.desiringgod.org/articles/who-is-the-church
12. 2 Corinthians 5:17
13. See John 3:1-21
14. See Ephesians 2:1-10
15. See Matthew 6:10
16. See 2 Corinthians 5:11-15
17. Ruth Haley Barton—*Pursuing God's Will Together*
18. See Matthew 28:19-20
19. See Mark 2:16-17
20. John 13:35
21. Matthew 6:10
22. See Matthew 22:37-40 and 28:19-20
23. Acts 2:42
24. See Mark 8:35

6. Don't Just Sing There

1. See Psalm 59:16, 98:1, and 100
2. See 2 Chronicles 5:11-14 and Psalm 136
3. Colossians 3:16
4. See Philippians 2:6-11; 1 Timothy 3:16; Ephesians 5:14; Colossians 1:15-20
5. https://www.christianity.com/church/church-history/timeline/1-300/sing-and-make-melody-to-god-11629579.html
6. Matthew 23:3
7. Matthew 23:11-12
8. Colossians 3:17 [emphasis added]
9. Hebrews 13:15-16

7. Give Yourself Away

1. https://www.jennieallen.com/blog/stop-hurrying-with-john-mark-comer
2. See John 16:12-15
3. 1 Corinthians 6:19-20a
4. https://www.ligonier.org/learn/articles/heidelberg-catechism-1563/

5. See Genesis 1 and 2
6. See Philippians 2:7 NIV
7. See 1 John 4
8. See Matthew 5:44
9. See Genesis 1:26-27
10. See John 3:16
11. See 2 Corinthians 5:11-21
12. Adele Calhoun - *The Spiritual Disciplines Handbook* - pg 146

8. Redefine Love

1. Mark 10:17
2. See John 3:14-15, 5:24, and 17:3
3. Mark 10:20
4. Mark 10:21a
5. https://www.christiantoday.com/article/god-is-love-understanding-the-3-different-words-for-love-in-the-new-testament/86282.htm for a helpful description of these New Testament definitions.
6. Mark 10:22
7. See 1 John 4:8,16
8. 1 John 4:7
9. 1 John 4:12
10. 1 John 4:17
11. Jeremiah 17:9 ESV
12. Exodus 20:6
13. See Colossians 3:23
14. For more reading on how to observe the Sabbath today, see *The Ruthless Elimination of Hurry* by John Mark Comer, *An Unhurried Life* by Alan Fadling, *Subversive Sabbath* by A.J. Swoboda, *Sabbath as Resistance* by Walter Brueggemann, and *The Common Rule* by Justin Earley,
15. See Genesis 1:26-31, John 3:16, Ephesians 2:10, and 1 Peter 2:9
16. See Ephesians 5:21-33
17. See Exodus 20:1-17 for the Ten Commandments
18. Psalm 94:11 ESV. Also see Psalm 139:4 and Matthew 6:8, 15:19
19. Matthew 5:48
20. 1 John 4:7b-8 [emphasis added]
21. See Genesis 1:27 and Romans 8:17
22. See John 15:1-15

9. Remember Who You Are

1. See Genesis 1:1
2. See John 1:29
3. See Mark 1:11
4. Genesis 1:31 [emphasis added]
5. See John 2:1-12
6. See Luke 19:1-10
7. See John 3:1-21
8. See Luke 8:2
9. See John 4:1-42
10. See Psalm 18:19
11. See Exodus 33:11, James 2:23
12. See Luke 10:38-42, John 11 and 12
13. See all of the Gospels and Acts
14. See Psalm 139:14, NIV
15. Michael Hyatt, the leadership and productivity guru, introduced me to this concept through his books and blog at www.michaelhyatt.com.

10. Name Your Idols

1. https://web.ics.purdue.edu/~drkelly/DFWKenyonAddress2005.pdf
2. https://www.christianheadlines.com/contributors/mikaela-matthews/union-theological-seminary-urges-its-students-to-confess-sins-to-plants.html
3. https://twitter.com/UnionSeminary/status/1174000941667880960
4. {$NOTE_LABEL} https://www.christianpost.com/news/union-seminary-mocked-for-having-students-confess-to-plants.html
5. John Eldredge, *Walking With God,* pg 82
6. https://web.ics.purdue.edu/~drkelly/DFWKenyonAddress2005.pdf
7. See Ephesians 6:12
8. See John 10:10 and 1 Peter 5:8
9. See Acts 17:24
10. See Acts 17:25
11. See Acts 17:28
12. See Deuteronomy 30:15-20
13. James 4:7
14. Deuteronomy 6:4
15. John 10:10
16. See Matthew 16:25, Mark 8:35, Luke 9:24
17. https://www.ignatianspirituality.com/ignatian-prayer/the-examen/
18. See Psalm 139, John 3:16
19. See Acts 4:12
20. Proverbs 18:10

21. See John 14:16b and Hebrews 13:5b

11. Embrace Your Suffering

1. Romans 8:28 NIV
2. Hebrews 12:2
3. John 9:2
4. John 9:3
5. See John 9:10
6. See John 9:26
7. See John 9:12
8. John 11:4
9. John 11:14b-15a
10. John 11:40
11. John 11:43
12. See John 11:35
13. Matthew 26:38
14. See Luke 22:44 ESV
15. Matthew 26:42
16. Matthew 26:44
17. See Matthew 26:45-46
18. See Colossians 1
19. See Revelation 21 and 22
20. See Hebrews 12:2
21. Job 1:8
22. Job 1:21
23. See Mark 10:17-23
24. See John 11:35
25. See Matthew 4:1-11
26. See Matthew 26:36-46, Mark 14:32-42, and Luke 22:39-46
27. Cornelius Plantinga, Jr. - *Not the Way It's Supposed To Be* - pg 10
28. See Revelation 21-22
29. 2 Chronicles 20:3
30. Nehemiah 1:3
31. See Nehemiah 1:4
32. Matthew 26:39
33. See Romans 8:28
34. See Romans 5:3-4
35. See James 1:2-4

12. Share The Gospel

1. https://dwillard.org/articles/live-life-to-the-full
2. See Ephesians 2:9-10
3. See Luke 4:16-21
4. See Acts 2:37
5. Acts 2:38
6. Acts 2:41
7. Stanley J. Grenz, David Guretzki, and Cherith Fee Nordling - *Pocket Dictionary of Theological Terms* - Pg 55
8. See John 17:1-5
9. John 12:28
10. See John 7:18, Romans 1:1-5, Ephesians 3:10-11, 1 Peter 4:11, and Jude 25
11. See John 17:20-26
12. Acts 17:28
13. https://www.opc.org/sc.html
14. D.A. Carson, "What Is the Gospel? – Revisited," in *For the Fame of God's Name: Essays in Honor of John Piper* - pg 158.
15. D. Martyn Lloyd-Jones - *Spiritual Depression: Its Causes and Cures* - pgs 20-21 [emphasis added]
16. See Romans 7 and 8

Epilogue

1. See Luke 22:42

Appendix

1. See Psalm 34:10
2. Walter Wangerin - *Whole Prayer* - pg 29
3. See Hebrews 4:12
4. See 2 Timothy 3:16-17
5. http://teilharddechardin.org/index.php/teilhards-quotes
6. See Matthew 16:25, Mark 8:35, Luke 9:24, John 12:25
7. See Revelation 21:1-5
8. See Matthew 28:18-20, Acts 1:8, 2 Corinthians 5:17-21